These Are the Words

These Are the Words

George Elliott Clarke
John B. Lee

First Edition

Hidden Brook Press
www.HiddenBrookPress.com
writers@HiddenBrookPress.com

Copyright © 2018 Hidden Brook Press
Copyright © 2018 Authors

All rights for poems revert to the author. All rights for book, layout and design remain with Hidden Brook Press. No part of this book may be reproduced except by a reviewer who may quote brief passages in a review. The use of any part of this publication reproduced, transmitted in any form or by any means, electronic, mechanical, photocopied, recorded or otherwise stored in a retrieval system without prior written consent of the publisher is an infringement of the copyright law.

These Are the Words
by George Elliott Clarke, John B. Lee

Cover Design – Richard M. Grove
Layout and Design – Richard M. Grove

Typeset in Garamond
Printed and bound in Canada
Distributed in USA by Ingram,
       in Canada by Hidden Brook Distribution

Library and Archives Canada Cataloguing in Publication

    These are the words / George Elliott Clarke, John B. Lee.

Poems.
ISBN 978-1-927725-55-9 (softcover)

    1. Canadian poetry (English)--21st century.

PS8293.1.T54 2018   C811'.608   C2018-901781-3

Table of Contents

The Gospel of Tobit
George Elliott Clarke

These Are the Words:
A contemplation of George Elliott Clarke's
The Gospel of Tobit – p. 3

Forewarning – *p. 11*
I – *p. 12*
II – *p. 17*
III – *p. 21*
IV – *p. 27*
V – *p. 30*
VI – *p. 34*
VII – *p. 39*
VIII – *p. 44*
IX – *p. 49*
X – *p. 52*
XI – *p. 56*
XII – *p. 61*
XIII – *p. 65*
XIV – *p. 68*

Bread, Water, Love
John B. Lee

The Elemental Is Monumental:
A contemplation of John B. Lee's
Bread, Water, Love – *p. 75*

Preface – *p. 81*
Bread, Water, Love – *p. 82*
Here in the Day – *p. 83*
Unmistakable Strangers – *p. 85*
Songs for a Bountiful Solitude – *p. 87*
Black Snow, Lost Light – *p. 89*
Cursing Under Water – *p. 92*
The Gift – *p. 94*
Not Nothing – *p. 96*
The Sculpture – *p. 99*
The Red-Tailed Hawk – *p. 101*
Willow-Want – *p. 103*
Nothing But Light – *p. 105*
Still Warm and Burning – *p. 107*
The Experiment – *p. 109*
I Watch the Lake on Morning's Christmas Eve – *p. 111*
Oh, Gentle Me – *p. 112*
He Only Does That When He's Thirsty for Danger – *p. 116*
What Awaits Me in the Sandwash – *p. 118*
The Black Hand Speaks – *p. 120*
Beyond the last sandbar – *p. 121*
Sunset in Dover, September 15, 2016 – *p. 123*
The Awakening – *p. 125*
Eros – *p. 127*
Darling, may I touch your pinkletink – *p. 128*
Were I – *p. 131*
Open – *p. 133*
When My Beloved Writes of Her Soul – *p. 134*
Last Evening – *p. 136*
On the Occasion of the Night of the Last Snow Moon – *p. 137*
Driving Home at Sundown – *p. 138*
Oh, my dark companion – *p. 140*
Erie Farne – *p. 143*

The Gospel of Tobit

George Elliott Clarke

These Are the Words:
A contemplation of George Elliott Clarke's
The Gospel of Tobit

Under the imprimatur of Hidden Brook Press, George Elliott Clarke's fascinating and very contemporary translation of *The Gospel of Tobit* appears for the first time in book form. Rendered into the living idiom of the streets, Clarke's lively poetic version takes its place alongside of Stephen Mitchell's *Gilgamesh,* Ted Hughes' *Tales of Ovid,* and Seamus Heaney's *Beowulf,* as an important example of ancient writing revivified from antiquity. One can find a rather flat and prosaic recent version of this text in the *Roman Catholic New American Bible* (July 27, 1970) under the title, "The Book of Tobit." This being one of the nine books of Apocrypha, it is placed between "Nehemiah" and "Esther" as chapter fourteen in the *Old Testament.* Referred to as being of the literary form of religious novel, it is also sometimes situated between historical books and those books considered to be part of the *wisdom* tradition. The original text was written in Aramaic around the second century B.C. For centuries this original text was lost, and the Greek translation served as the primary source for most impressions.

With the courage of early English translator William Tyndale and the poetic verve of the contemporary Laureate, Clarke embraces the erotic and sometimes vulgar language of poets from Catullus through Layton and all those brave souls who defy the squeamish sensibilities of the prude.

If you doubt for a moment that you are in the hands of a poetic voice worthy of the task, consider for example this early verse from chapter I:

To widows slumped, weepy in black weeds,
and to orphans starved for smiles and candy,
and to heathens now deeming Israel's God
"the baddest Top Dog,"
rendered I purple satin purses, blinding with silver.

    The penultimate line of this stanza - *the baddest Top Dog* - establishes this particular translation, as one to be reckoned with - *the baddest Top Dog* - indeed! Consider the accumulation of strong verbs in the opening salvo – *cussed-out, sweet-talked, and spat* - Never! This story inspired by the moral rectitude of the protagonist in this passage comes hurling at the reader like a volley of expletives. And the energy of this translation is sustained in verse after verse. The moral father, the dutiful son, the doting mother, the exile, the love interest, the hot sex, the demon, the angel, the bride, the orphan, all here in this sometimes steamy rendering of marital consummation.
    The relationship between prayer and poem, between divine revelation and the written word is embraced and celebrated by Clarke in his honouring of poetry in lines like:

The sun's hours are a journey of *Music*—
as utopian as a poem.

And:

"Lord, who hath copyright on Thee?
Every honest poem seeks to read Thy heart."

And then again much later very near the end of the book:

This news—as old as soil—
is hollered from poem to poem.

How prisoners' prayers are blues;
inmates' *matins* are mother's milk mourned.

Since the word *Deuteronomy* has the ad verbum translation "these are the words," one might say of George Elliott Clarke's *Gospel of Tobit,* "these are the *right* words," and mean it. Coleridge said of poetry that poetry is "the best words in their best order." And sometimes such words as:

Alone in her bed, Sarah awakes
and strokes her pussy—
not too much, not galore,
for, to frig oneself is to ape the devil.

Stops she; prays she:

"I lost my breathing to gasping;
I lost my holding to grasping:
Love is a living power—
as unmanageable as *Death*."

may make the odd reader blush, but they are the *mots justes* of this moment in the work, and we mustn't forget Shakespeare's medlars or John Donne's "For God's sake hold your tongue, and let me love," lest we lapse into a time before the fruit of the tree of knowledge gave man and woman the judgment of angels and poets, priests and gods.

John B. Lee
Poet Laureate of the city of Brantford in perpetuity
Poet Laureate of Norfolk County for life

The Gospel of Tobit

*For El Hajj Malik El Shabazz
(1925-65)*

"*Beauty, beauty... What's beauty anyway?*"
—Dany Laferrière,
How to Make Love to a Negro without Getting Tired

Forewarning

This *Gospel of Tobit* is actually an excerpt from an epic-in-progress, *Canticles*, of which *Canticles I* has already appeared (in two volumes, 2016-2017). *Canticles II* will present, once completed (God willing), my rewriting of selected scriptures, based on my sense of how African peoples in Western European and American bondage and then (relative) freedom scrupled (bothered) to interpret texts that must have first come to them, being illiterate, as a set of quixotic and chaotic tales. I beg your indulgence: My point is not *Blasphemy*, but reverence for how the oral and the aural became *spiritual(s)*—immaculate *Mystery*; pencils towing leaden words; doled out splatters of ink, doleful, askew; domestic, homely lettering; a gusty *Bible* as navigable as a wreck; the unwinding whispers, sounding sobs, and invisible moans of such a listing text....

This work reflects inspiration gleaned from *The New Oxford Annotated Apocrypha, 3rd Edition*, ed. Michael D. Coogan; assoc. eds., Marc Z. Brettler, Carol A. Newsom, Pheme Perkins (Oxford, 2001). I have effected rewrites of scholarly translations. My "Gospel" follows the Hebraic-but-Anglicized original as much as a shadow follows the sun.

I've been assisted in my "transcription" by my usual, customary, excellent editor, Mr. Paul Zemokhol. As is normal, I alone am guilty for the sins—herein—of omission and commission.

I do thank Richard Grove (Tai) and that forever-alive Poet Laureate John B. Lee for inciting this work, I mean, catalyzing the publication. I say, "Whoopee" for their whoop-ass aesthetics /ethics.

For any reader who feels ire for my darkling inkling, or who takes umbrage at my poetical encumbering of quasi-biblical numbers, I pass along the good news that I'm mortal. Just turn the page: I'm *History*.

George Elliott Clarke
Toronto (Ontario)
8 janvier mmxviii

I

      Though all my kin were either cussed out—
or sweet-talked—
to slaughter, giddily,
their very children, their heirs,
in homage to the gold-forged goat
dictator Jeroboam had the gall to erect—
humongous atop a Galilee hill—
hear loudly that I spat, "Never!"

      Piqued, caravan'd I to Jerusalem,
ferrying fiestas of apples, figs,
pomegranates, tangerines,
and heading a train of milk-dripping cows
and wool-weighted sheep:

All to dodge State-forced *Blasphemy*;
denote myself a capital citizen.

      To *comme-ci-comme-ʒa* theologians—
those misanthropic, yet anus-drilling priests—
brought I tithes of bread, tithes of *vino*,
to urge on angered-up harangues,
spitting fire at the baby-deficit *Tyranny*.

      Bright coins, 7-years-hoarded, I now splurged—
to wine-and-dine bags-o-bones;
to prop up once-crumpled cripples.

      To widows slumped, weepy in black weeds,
and to orphans starved for smiles and candy,
and to heathens now deeming Israel's God
"the baddest Top Dog,"
rendered I purple satin purses, blinding with silver.

       I resolved on *Charity* because
papa's in a grave nursing worms:
I'm an orphan—
a student of *Suffering*.

       When Assyria-shackled was I,
chained down as a "nigger serf" in Nineveh,
Disgust roiled my heart when I witnessed Jews
yum-yum the Gentiles' swine-carved tidbits.
(I did prefer gut-gnawing *Hunger*
to ever guttling this Aryan offal.)

       I spurned boozed-up *Lust*
and all pig-tainted pastries.

       Because God backed my refusal of *Gentility*—
i.e., of genteel *Obedience*
to those kiddy-homicides pleasing an oligarch—
I became painstakingly the *eminence grise*
for King Semihemi—
and kept up—kept stock of—
his chattel, wine, tools, and silks.

       Semihemi's beard swam about his chin,
brimmed at his mouth.

Note: Dude muff-dived so many ladled-out laps,
nymphs' groans could've roused even a eunuch!

       Sho' nuff, one plump-assed, big-jugged maid—
her taut cunt snugged tight to his eel—
jerked the monarch to his grave
via a snag—a catch—in his heart.

       Now King Scarab whipped up *Crime:*
Hurled he helpless down the *sans-culottes*
under his gangbanging, royal swords.

(*Poverty?* Smell the plague-stinking slum;
ogle the gaggle of gaunt thieves, jailed,
then forced to watch their gallows go up.)

Yes, shitty was the moolah I pocketed;
but I was snow-white in *Honesty*—
even according to unpublished accounts.

Everywhere, always,
The Treasurer is Judge.

(*Banking* is anthemic ingestion
and/or operatic liquidation.)

I'd hunt down bargain goods,
scavenging all of Media;
then, sales stashed, deposited I
profits with Gabby, bro to Gabri—
10 sacks snazzy with dazzling coin.

(Robbers beset highways:
I feared my silver'd prove honey to hijackers.)

During the Scarab* Administration,
if I viewed any dead Hebrew—Believer—
a cadaver frothing maggots—
dumped over the city walls—
or left to weep poison into a well,
I'd go out at night and gouge that somebody
a proper grave.

I'd also chop down the neck-dangled—
or crowbar the crucified from splintering wood—
then spade sand over their grimaces.

---

* *Trump.*

  (Many an ecclesiastical peasant—
stronzo, cafone—
would suffer a folk-art x-ing;
many an olive-drab prole—
some home-taught carpenter—
would either dance from gallows
or splay quadriplegic, spiked to a cross.)

  I'd sneak through shadows and cart
killed-off Israelites to undetectable, desert burials,
so that King Scarab couldn't command
his miserable soldiery to shit
on the open eyes, or shit
in the open mouths.

  But an envious perp gossiped
my *Charity* to the devil-ministered king.
He bade cops come lariat my neck.

  Les flics toted off my goods—
"plunder"—in jumbo carts.
The arithmetic was clear:
I had to make myself scarce. Pronto!

My weird *Joy*? That my wife, Anna,
mom to our son, Tobias,
could share my exile.

  But inside 40 days,
that douche-bag Scarab
got infiltrated by icepicks,
while bedding his son's wife.

  A point drilled through his temple;
his blood freshly raped the wailing *femme*.
Another prick poked through his anus,
disemboweling him awesomely,
twisting and dicing his entrails.
(The white-faced fucker got a black-ditch asshole!)

The Assassin-Prince vamoosed—
vacated—to Ararat.
Next, Prince Easy-Harder plunked down his ass,
enthroned.

Subsequently, my nephew, Herky,
now became the comptroller of the *Bourse*.

Quickly, a joint Treasurer,
with Herky, in Nineveh, was I.

I went from *Disgrace* to *Power*,*
while Scarab petrified in a peat bog,
and Semihemi seethed with maggots in grave dirt,
sunflower roots threading darkly his yellow hair.

[Sechelt (British Columbia) 14 *août* mmxvi]

---

* *Thus, executing—metaphorically—a parachute jump into a volcano....*

II

      At home, my wife Anna and lad, Tobias,
dished up a feast, and I reclined to recuperate,
i.e., dine.

      A rye-bread & purple-wine (*Manischewitz*) Renaissance!

      I planned to settle into music—
as if lounging in bed.

      But before fork or spoon could meet my mouth,
I tasked Tobias to seek a scrawny Jew—
to seat at our table and sup.

      Instead, Tobias scurried back, shouting
"A Hebrew's slain and's slung
mid the swollen midden.

      "Gripped violently by a biting rope,
the victim's face shows bloody craquelure.
Huddled in his own shadow he be."

      (Ravens exculpate the dead easily:
The sinner, deceased, makes the raptors' *Rapture*.)

      I quit the table, the music, the food,
the wine, the belly-trembling ballerinas,
and skedaddled to the dump—
clutched up the corpse—
a teen's body—
out the redoubled cesspool where his bleeding
drained down to the sewer:
Ochre stars lit up his bleached, grey face.

      I snuck the cadaver back into the palace,
to parlour it among wine bottles
until midnight could shroud burial.

(Can a dead dreamer demur as maggots smack,
taking his flesh as lard cake?

Prophet Amos was politic to observe,
"Suppers spoil beside the murdered:
Tears ruin sweet-meats and salt down wine.")

Freshly scoured,
broke I ground for the new corpse,
while dogs bayed about, growled.

A meagre lamp's light staged my gestures—
the shadows of *Love*—
the furtive *Allegory*.

(*Darkness* stretches over us:
Earth gets pitched onto our faces.)

A spy chortled at my *Charity*:
"Ain't Tobias a dog's carcass fit for a gutter?
He's gone back to shovelling out holes
for contraband executionees!

(His libations? Wormwood and/or bilge.)"

After sweating over the lynched youth,
I chose to bed down outdoors,
but kept my upturned face bared,
wanting wind and dew to launder
what was clammy or damp.

Constellations burned up the night—
though I was insensible.

Faces levitated before my sleep-locked eyes—
glimpses of The Dead.

    Ravens flitted to-and-fro
o'er my star-lit litter,
but doused my drowsing visage
with acidic guano—
damaging jets—that,
liquefied by my nightmare-brewed sobs,
seeped gall into my eyes,
glomming up a white film—rheum—
that blanked out my vision.

Avian defecate ate into my eyes' sockets....

    As dawn light licked pale upon my eyelids,
and birdsong detonated a denotating lingo—
my tongue nicked at bird-dung speckling my teeth.

    My eyes oped,
but no doctor, no ointment, could lighten
my facing sudden, ravenous darkness.

    Herky, pitying me, tended me two years,
then left for Elymais.

    Those four years of blindness, I was
as glacial as is grass, growing.
Sluggish blood chugged through my jugular.

    I experienced the claustrophobia
of an insomniac's coma.

    Anna salvaged—foraged—coins
by patching neighbours' clothes
or scouring way their filth.

    One glad patron paid off with a gold coin—
and a white goat righteous for throat-cutting.

    Occasionally came slushy strawberries
and gin sloshing cucumbers,
and wine-soaked tobacco.

      When Anna brought home the goat,
it began to bleat and bah.
I worried the commotion signalled *Theft*.
I admonished Anna, "Return this stolen critter!
Its flesh must be a disease....
We'll gobble soupy lettuce, wormy mackerel, instead."

      Anna answered: "We ain't betrayed!
I wasn't beguiled!
Do not be to me *Frustration* and *Faithlessness*!

My needles won us needful gold and goat.

Why don't you *see* this creature and this coin
as Divine reward for your own righteous *Charity*—
to inter a costly horde of cadavers?

      "Oy! Must you trade sunlight for shit?"

[Sechelt (British Columbia) 14 *août* mmxvi]

III

        "Because my forebears were bastoods,*
kicking at Thy Decalogue,
O Lord, Thou bashest em good!

Their cash conveyered into cunts' pockets!
Nasty, they basted in Europe's dungeons.
Their gilded percentages, seemingly mint,
flaked off, showing virtual turds,
£s worth less than hen-scratch—
penny-ante crap.

        "Thou, O God, art never gypped,
never swindled, eh?
Thou ensurest sinners cringe and cramp;
chow down on copious gobs
of yellow-green phlegm;
savour salty snot.

        "Lawd, if I sin, just rip out my heart
and trample my soul into Hell's inferno!"

        While Tobit wept his elegy,
crimping, cross-legged in ash,
his stalled wheelchair also looking decrepit—
derelict (like Kafka's humanoid cockroach)—
Sarah, daughter to Miguel—
at Ecbatana, in Media—
sobbed prodigiously over her 7 uselessly white weddings
to 7 suave suitors,

cos all of em terminated in 7 *de facto* suicides.

---

* *A Three Mile Plains (NS) pronunciation....*

      Sarah's nuptials counted a regiment of martyrs—
7 penises lopped,
7 craniums chopped,
14 shanks and shins cropped to bone—
all dockings done by demonic Asmodeus
to forbid any lad to swoon over Sarah,
not even to attain the stage of fondling—
when the frilly bodice of a filly
unlaces,
allowing a man's lips to sip
chocolate nipple and milky tit.

      Sarah's 7 suitors were studies
in photo-realist Gothic—
apropos Caravaggio.

      As his tongue lapped at bones,
strung still with tasty gristle,
Asmodeus' lips smooched lustily.

      Sarah's suitors were 7 expired fiancés,
not actual grooms,
just 7 gory boy bellies and crotches.

      But it wasn't Sarah's fault (or Eve's)
that Asmodeus lusted to slick his defiling prick
in-and-out her awesomely muscled, squeezing orifice;
to tussle in bed as if in a trap;
to split her smoky diamond;
to stud the spicy, sassy, *b-i-t-c-h*,
stuffing her muff amid satin—
so as to explicate the Latin
of *cunnilingus* and *fellatio*, *et cetera*.

      Asmodeus was a hands-on,
red-handed, red-eyed cutthroat—
a diabolical cannibal.

No knife could've cut
the stink of his excrement,
his very thought—
the odor of squalor marinated in cess,
a grisly pollution.

He had the will to chafe—
to pry Sarah's thighs like a horse's mouth.
She'd realize—finally—
a virgin's unwilling widening,
"fo' an' aft."

Boldface, her maid chastised Sarah:
"You gripe and pound me with your slipper
just cos no man pounds your *belle-chose*—
to plug that awful gap with offspring.

"Then again, you butcher each groom
before his cock can slide twixt your gloomy shanks."

Guilt groaned in Sarah's marrow.
Her beauty compelled Asmodeus to guillotine
young men's penises,
to nick necks,
and scrape his teeth on thigh bones.

Sarah was as shakeable as is rain in wind.
She shook like a salt-shaker in a peasant's hand.

Never'd her thin gams part for her hubby's lance!
Never'd she gasp a wife's gruesome tears,
as the totem of a newborn—
the fresh skull ripping her like a knife,
as, urgent for air, to breathe,
lunges forth the blood-and-feces-slicked sinner.

Sorrowing, Sarah loosed the brine of her urine.
She struck the floor even before her piss or tears could.

Quick, the virgin chose to noose her neck.
Out of ribbons and sashes, she knotted the lasso.

But God nudged Sarah toward *Philosophy*:

"Should I asphyxiate myself from the ceiling candelabra,
so my strangled breath catches in my gullet,
my papa—Miguel—will be mocked:
'His only beloved daughter has hanged herself!'
He'd become a melancholic alcoholic;
vomit blood when not swilling red wine—
some ultra-violet, black-timbered *pinot noir*.
I'd push my papa down to Hell
due to his unstinting sobbing
over my cradle-robbing self-destruction.

Instead, let me shrivel
away in hunger, and die—
bereft of food as I am of *Love*."

Her face a shadow-dappled hieroglyphic,
and stretching her hands toward an upper window,
Sarah prayed beseechingly:

"Blessèd God, free me from this slaughterhouse bridal chamber—
this white room dressed for butchers or morticians—
and the scarlet *Disgrace* that stains me.

Am I ice,
never to be enflamed by a man like coal?"

Like meteors crossing a night sky,
darkling words sparkled her internal murk.

"O Master, I'm no daughter
taken in *Adultery*;
though I've wed now 7,
no man hath defiled me.
My pulse is untainted.
Never have I fetched at *Lechery*.
No trenchant plough has grooved
my shallow canal.

A fallow *Beauty* in a gore-sallow madhouse,
all my suitors are perished,
their grandiose faces gone to crematoria
(a blaze of worms);
their scarlet waterspouts of groins—
all surgically split up—
configure a grotesque trinity.

Never has the sweat of their black backs
trickled upon my ivory haunches.

Why shall I breathe further?"

      Pitying Sarah, God dispatched the Angel Raphael
to exorcise—expunge—Asmodeus
from her bridal chamber—
to clear out that odious and obstinate *Infestation*—
to free Sarah so she could wife Tobias—
and post a full-length mirror over the bed
to treasure ogling two joined figures,
the *Oreo* torsos reflected therein—
the white heat and hiss of sanctified coupling—
the pianissimo, venous hum* of spending....

---

* Cf. Suzette Mayr.

(Tobias must breed Sarah,
so that she may savour
the avalanche of a lover's breathing
tumbling down as they tremble
mid gusting sheets:
Her sex made—at last—a fertile terminus.)

And God also bade Raphael
to clear from Tobit's eyes that white film
opaquing the sun.

So it was that, simultaneously,
as Tobit exited his courtyard for his mansion,
his household wheelchair tick-tocking,
whickering, over marble tiles,
so did Sarah, that frond of lace,
quit her accursed bridal chamber,
that consecration of demon-bloodied linens.

(Note: The sun-gripped sunflower
rips down night.
Sight its seedy, yellow murk
amid shriveling daylight.

Best pray to enjoy the close-up
of the newborn,
before thou closeth the never-long-distance
to thy just-dug grave!

Extras, we're all extras,
in everyone else's life.)

[Sechelt (British Columbia) 14 & 15 *août* mmxvi]

IV

        Tobit reflects, "I've asked God
to kill me—a living SNAFU—ASAP.
Well, only a fire is forever young.
I'd best tell Tobias, my son,
to retrieve the *decad* of silver-stuffed sacks,
parked with Gabby
at Rages in Media—
a decade back."

        Tobit summons Tobias:

"When I'm done, wretched upon my pall,
that estate of static dirt,
inter me piously as Scripture commands,
and respect thy mama always.
Remember her milk that nourished thee
and her womb that shaped thee
and floated thee,
tucked away safe.

When she too has exhausted breath,
lay her reverently beside me,
so we're twined, almost serpentine.

        "Gift my surplus to the desperate,
and never cut eyes or suck teeth
while being exemplarily eleemosynary.
Extinguish our cash in distinguished *Charity*.

        "But don't imitate the governance of whores—
truckling to the wealthy and the wicked—
brown-nosing, cock-sucking....

        "Alms-gifting defies the grave
and entrenches, instead, our memory.

"Forego all *Fornication!*
Ply thy limbs in no sty
as brittle—or supple—as a spinster's sex.
Do not woo a foreign woman
(kin to Delilah):
She mates like a mare in must—
as careless as an inferno,
so she dribbles drool from her sucking lips,
swears to glue her genitals to thine.

"Filch no strange *pachole*—
her open-jawed cunt,
her clitoris like an incisor,
switching her ass like a glutton twitching his tongue.

"(Due to their palpitating guts,
intellectuals picture themselves as ramping stallions
pumping at the rumps of snorting fillies,
their phalli so frenzying the females,

their henna'd toes, their sandal'd heels,
kick apart their stalls—
their scandalous beds.)

"To have the unspoiled spice of a spouse,
always take a wife from among our kin.

"Do not refuse a wife chosen from among
our people's daughters.
Love our young ladies, lest their bodies go moot.

"To spurn thine own kind is akin
to active *Lassitude*,
and the lazy thinking of the lazy
breeds *Famine* and *Infertility*.

"Be as plush—and plain—as water.

"Only the sinful merit *Extinction*!

"Avoid Hades."

[Ljubljana (Slovenia) 20 & 21 *août* mmxvi]

V

       Tobit recounts, to Tobias, his banking—
with Gabby, son of Gabard—
of 10 potato sacks flooded with coins like silver shrimp,
moony, dismally dazzling.

       Tobias will fetch the currency,
but he wonders, "How will Gabby know
me as your son?
How will I reconnoiter the road to Media?"

       "Tell Gabby that you've come for my half,
that he and I divvied from the whole sum,
that he's held for me now 20 years.

       "Hire a scrupulous, meticulous guide.
I'll satisfy his wages once you've returned—
whole and hearty."

       Tobias now took on a thin black man—
lanky as an Eritrean sprinter—
who claimed knowledge of Media.
including Gabby's whereabouts....

       (As Tobias parted from the sable man—
as gaunt and dark as a licorice strand—
he glimpsed the stranger's Adonis profile
creep into shadow—
like a statue overtaken by dusk,
its dead face averted
from a revolutionary, insurgent blaze.)

       The bony, moose-tint man
gave his name as "Raphael"—
but did not i.d. himself as God's angel.

　　　　As if a G.P.S., Raphael now instructs Tobias,
"It's a two-night trek to reach Rages
(up in the mountains),
beyond the plains where sits Ecbatana.

　　　"We'll traverse labyrinthine bulrushes,
plus unhesitant blizzards of sand,
plus all those blank spots or ruins
that *History* once knew as pastoral."

　　　Before setting out,
Tobias intros Raphael to Tobit,
who elects to test the Falasha Jew's cool intellect,
in case it reveals a seditious,
incinerated, gone-ashen, now chilling *Theology*.

　　　Raphael exclaims, "Joyous salutations!"
But the blind man retorts,
"*Joy*? Impossible for me!
I live in darkness—like the dead."

　　　Raphael smiles: "If faithful to Lord God,
Mr. Tobit, I wager He'll repeal this curse."

　　　Tobit shrugs: "I've prayed and prayed,
but God sends no answer, no light....
Tell me, Raphael, can you guide Tobias to Media?"

　　　"I know all the routes, all the rivers.
and the compass pinpoints where one's at—
even when one's lost!

We'll easily locate Media—
where lightning winds up as rainbows."

　　　Now, the blind elder must needs ascertain
Raphael's genealogy:
"Who are your people?"

31

"God's people:
That branch of Israel that's strayed
among vineyards,
where the sun draws out unblanching *Comeliness*.

We are vintners among sunflowers
(those imitation stars):
Wine inks our epitaphs."

Tobit nods, reassured:
"Well, your people are my people—old-stock!

"I'll pay 1 drachma per day, plus costs;
return Tobias safely,
and I'll double your receipt."

Once Raphael exits, Tobit tells Tobias,
"Raphael will be a spur and a shield for thee."

Tobias now kissed his mama, Anna, goodbye.
But she shakes, a-fearing for Tobias.
She dreads the possible annihilation now—
decades later—
of her dilated cervix.

"Why heap your living gold self
prostrate over dead, dull metal,
that drab, dingy silver?"

Tobit consoles Anna:
"Hush! Our eyes will glitter
when we behold Tobias's return.
This Raphael is the inkling of an angel."

Anna frets still:

"The two will pass through olive trees
gone black with night,
with stars a-rustle.

Thus, chills've got purchase on my heart—
that worksite—
of pounding and pressing,
and now carrying cold,
each of my cells now searing me
like frost—
or a splinter of ice."

[Jeruzalem (Slovenia) 21 *août* mmxvi]

VI

      Anna ceased (for now) her tears.

Likewise, as soon as rain rounds off April,
May arrives, beaming,
and soon the greenery throbs,
and the preening grass purrs.

      Raphael—that offbeat, wiry, *shayner yid*—
departed alongside Tobias;
and then Tobit's frisky, Bichon Frise pup, Chloé,
abandoned her master's wheelchair
and scrambled after Tobias,
yapping alongside the two wayfarers,
but not very far:

Chloé could not forsake Massa Tobit's milk and meat!

      Tobias and Raphael wended miles end-ways—
until the disguised angel and his companion
camped alongside the Tigris River
as night dropped down,
and their fire cooked up tar-black coffee,
and the melodramatic flares scared off lions.

      Looming above their miniscule blaze,
gloomed the moon's grotesque yellow,
gulping night's cold, black velvet.

      Come dawn cold, Tobias thrust his dusty feet
into the chilly river current,
to scour and soothe heels, soles, toes.
He heard the sibilant grating of pebbles
nuzzled by surf,
and sighed.

But, goddamn! A fish as large as a fence-post
swallowed whole his left foot!

The gargantuan fish had a curious beige tinge
as it leapt from the turbid, pallid element.

Tobias screeched, panicked! He saw his left foot
disappear into the marine monster's maw.

Its labial and dental clutch felt as rough and sharp as gravel.

Hearing Tobias's shock,
Raphael sped to his aid, but chided him,
"Fool!
Geez, in this fish, there's *Salvation*!
Step back onto the riverbank
and drag the finny thing with you.
Once it perishes, your foot will slide free."

Shortly, the non-amphibious "fellatrix" died,
liberating Tobias's once-trapped foot.

Next, Raphael commanded Tobias,
"Dissect the dinosaur;
grab its heart, liver, gall, guts;
discard the intestines."

Raphael's brusque authority forbade
shillyshallying and second-guessing.

(Indeed, a poet also airs *Truth*,
but it must flutter out of reach—
unless an intellectual, like Tobias—
has nets for ears.)

At Media, Raphael lectured Tobias:

"Burn these piscicultural bits—
liver and heart—
so that anyone infested demonically
will inhale the fumes
and repel, vomiting, the havoc-wreaking devil.

"Also, you can concoct a potion
from the gall that, smeared over filmy eyes,
revives sight in once-dull orbs."

Tobias fretted,
asking himself,
"Is this *fauxonry—Deception*?
Or *tolletry—Magic*?"

Shortly, Raphael pointed Tobias to Miguel's home,
and prophesied, intriguingly,
"Miguel's daughter—Sarah—who belongs
to your lineage (*Genealogy*)—
will become your breathtaking bride....

Before Tobias could demur,
Raphael added, "Sarah is singularly virtuous and *bella*.
She's no *graillon*—
no slut or slattern—
reeking of rancid wine.
No, she wafts the perfume of sunlight.
The down on her arm? Ivory fur.
Her Siamese-cat eyes burn coppery.
At love, her hair will cover you
like new, fresh, tender fronds.

"Check: Marriage to Sarah
is the theological precondition for *Harmony*."

Now Tobias cavilled bitterly:

"Isn't Sarah, notoriously, 7 times a widow,
who's wept over 7 dead grooms,
all slain in her bridal chambers?
Ain't she better with a hearse
than with a baby carriage?

"I'm my parents' sole hope
for a respectful burial:
A marriage bed with Sarah
will prove a deathbed for me,
and aggrieve my parents,
whom, once dead, strangers will fling into ditches."

Raphael interrupted Tobias:
"All breathing risks *Disappointment*.

Anyhow, thou shalt fuck Sarah—kindred—
this exact night.

"Yet, to avoid the grisly fates of her first 7 suitors,
thou shalt enter Sarah's bridal chambers,
conjure smoke—incense—from the dry fish guts,
so that her inhalation of these fumes
drives out Asmodeus,
that grizzled, sadistic gaffer—
that perverse tool craving salt, sugar, cigarettes, *Sex*,
which has so lusted for Sarah's *riemurasia*,*
the monster hashed up her husbands.

---

* *Finnish: Treasury.*

      "But before thou can stud the filly—
in snorting, wheezing horseplay—
and breed thy brats,
before thou can undergo undiminished undulations—
to screw in her nick, her nether throat—
thrusting into her jerking, twerking,
sweet-smelling cunt,
I mean, make her thy wife and blast her *Virginity*—
so she squeezes and pressures
thy dick, cranking up thy spunk—
immaculate ejaculate—

thou must beg God for *Mercy*.

      "Understand: Tobias, Sarah has been pledged
to be thy helpmate since Eve was made Adam's,
and thou shalt drink up wine and pour out songs,
and dine on lamb and feed on *Love*."

      Suddenly, Tobias feels *Love* occupy his heart—
a pure *Love*—
for Sarah's stirred neither his eyes
nor his loins.

      Suddenly, he wants her as desperately
as dying men want *Life*.

      Tobias muses:

Breathless breathing,
Deathless breathing,
That's us—in bed.

[Jeruzalem (Slovenia) 22 *août* mmxvi]

VII

   Crossing a blazing pond, Tobias
and Raphael trek into Ecbatana,
and seek out Miguel,
that meatified gent,
that dude flush with plush (fat, girth, heft).

   Miguel spied out Tobias's kinship instantly:
The plump chap told wife Edna,
"This youth mirrors the blind invalid, Tobit,

save that he's healthy."

   Still, Edna questioned the arrivants.
The subtle angel piped up, elaborated,
"I'm Raphael, in the employ of Tobias.
We're descended from Napthali,
those Nineveh exiles."

   Edna echoed Miguel:
"Tobias, thou must be kin to Tobit:
you're virtually his twin."

   "I'm Tobit's only child, his son."

   "Is Tobit's health fair—
despite blindness, his wheelchair?"

   "My papa breathes, and his exhaled words
have commanded my coming to Miguel."

   Miguel exclaimed, "O blessings to thee,
and healing to Tobit,
struck so miserably blind

(as if maltreated by docs)."

Now, Miguel wept for *Nostalgia*, *Neuralgia*,
for misfortunes that stymie even pious Believers.

And Edna wept.

And Sarah, joining her parents, also wept.

Tobias didn't—couldn't—weep. He eyed Sarah,
and Raphael's prophecy succeeded:
He loved—at once—her slender, neon-white legs,
her sweet breasts—like two twin coconuts in shape,
and like coconuts' innards (he guessed) in colour—
her red lips and black hair,
her gold-tint eyes, her white-cream complexion,
her aroma like fresh milk....

Miguel bade that a ram be cut across the neck
and cut open at belly,
and spitted lickety-split,
with a rosy apple stuck
in its silently screaming jaws.

Once bathed, Raphael and Tobias
sat cross-legged on mats,
to grind their molars on rare ram testicles—
and slurp mauve wine.
Then, Tobias addressed Raphael:
"It is true—just as you said: I love Sarah.
Please ask Miguel to let her be my wife."

Miguel overheard Tobias's request,
and twisted his own head slowly,
nixing Tobias's impulse:

"I can't let you wed Sarah,
though I'd like to—as kin:
You're practically her brother,
Tobias, but I gotta admit
that 7 suitors,

then 7 grooms,
said, "I do," to Sarah;
but before they could "do" her—
I mean, couple with her as a wife—
did all die, losing big head and little head.

    Edna was also a downer:

"Frankly, to marry is to bargain on a boning, eh?
A wife readies her treasure chest for rummaging;
or she opes her hot pot for a man's spoon
to froth and stir until her juices boil over....

But Sarah's affairs all end in homicides—
as if her swains were virgin suicides."

    Sarah sat, blanching, silent, through these elegies.
But Tobias swore,
"'I'll starve; I'll thirst; but I'll not leave this mansion
until I've satisfied my rights as Sarah's husband!"

    Miguel: "Well, consider thyselves duly married,
by my word, in accord with Mosiac decree.
Lad, take Sarah now and enjoy her as familiarly
as parents map the newborn's body.
I bless thee unreservedly."

    Tobias winked at quaking Sarah:

She worried sore that this *l'amour*
would also conclude in *la mort*.

    Miguel summoned Sarah and Tobias
to his study, where ink and papyrus
awaited his drafting—
with Edna and Raphael as sworn witnesses—
of Sarah's (8th) formal, marriage contract.

(The torn-up remains of the first 7 contracts
littered the waste basket.)

Once the Mosiac Law was scripted—
in Coptic calligraphy—
official was the marriage
and sorrowfully ecstatic was the feast—
like a funereal—if drink-rich—wake.

Miguel shouted that he had "a happy thirst,"
but Tobias couldn't afford to be
as ripe as a grog-headed pirate.
He had an 8th of a maple-sugar loaf,
and seasoned it with cheese....

After *Bliss: Dread.*

Miguel bade Edna prepare the bridal bed
(for the 8th time)
and lead shaky Sarah therein.
Mother and daughter sobbed,
their tears salty, bountiful:

Must Sarah's 8th husband—a kinsman—
be carved into head cheese, prairie oysters, and sirloin?

But Edna snuffed her tears—
enough to command Sarah to *Courage*,
and to advise her (again):

"The taste of him will be like lime—
and/or Champagne vinegar
or sweet-and-sour milk....
When he's in you—or when you're atop him—
the wobbling's double—like ship and sea—
and you warble—or you shout glad woes—
ecstatic, to cancel—I pray—any curse.

"I pray this time your wedding night
is only exultation,
not a new extinction."

[Jeruzalem (Slovenia) 23 *août* mmxvi]

VIII

       The wedding orgies tapered off,
while night ambled in, umber after amber—
that ruby-gold-copper-liquid sunset....

Now, Tobias posted, dauntless, to the bridal chamber—
that seven-time death-camp, haunting, haunted.

       The groom checked a pocket in his white robe,
fingered the bizarre fish heart and guts (liver),
all at the ready,
while Sarah shivered abed,
quivering under the albescent satin
(her skin flaunting the fragile hue
of an apple-blossom-tinted butterfly).
Aye, she lusted for her 8th husband,
but also dreaded his plausible, instant butchering,
that, before his jabbing phallus could puncture
her tight, girlish hymen—

Tobias'd be skewered quick as he,
his manhood,
unsheathed.

       Instead, Tobias grinned as he unpocketed
dried fins, gills, and scattered em in the flames,
so that a fishy smell pervaded the fumes.
This queer offal burned to a pale powder.

       The piscine aroma expelled Asmodeus!
Cat-piss-acrid elements assaulted his nostrils.
The sketchy demon's eyes squirmed and squirted blood
that turned to embers.
He skedaddled,
and the newlyweds heard his choked-off, banshee howl
as his pallid phantom—
as pale as a faded deed—
scooted up the chimney

and out-flapped dragon-wings
to flit to the far shadow of a pyramid.

    (The Holy Land is the perfect dump
for miscellaneous, irreligious junk:
It is bronze wastes, blood-watered.)

    Via Astral-Projection,
Raphael pursued the panting monster,
bound the male thing with iron bands,
sawed off his rigid, two-foot-long cock,
and shoved him, bawling, neath a Sphinx.

    Asmodeus was dethroned, defanged, unmanned:
This is how one abolishes parasites!

    Exceedingly glad for this triumphant *Alchemy*,
Tobias slid into bed beside Sarah,
who winced and gasped at the touch of his penis
against her right leg,
as he turned towards her,
but he merely clasped her right hand,
and said, "Before we love,
let's give thanks that *Heraldry* equals *History*."*

    Still skittish, if not squeamish,
Sarah nodded gravely at Tobias,
who intoned,
"Lord God, Thou maketh Adam
and then maketh Eve to be his comfort.
From their coupling, all of *Humanity*
has had descent.
Now I, sweet Lord, take my kinswoman,
Sarah, as my bride;
so that we may mother children,
and deserve to live long a couple."

---

* *Her and His.*

The newlyweds concluded, harmoniously,
"*Bravo! Bravissimo!*"

Tobias tossed back the sheet
to tongue and wet Sarah's slit,
relishing the meaningful tremble
and dimpling of liquid over her labia.

He had to survey intimately the vineyard
and apiary and dairy of her body.

As Tobias tongued Sarah's quim,
poising at the brink of *Struggle*,
he took a swig of wine
so that the surging bottle
lunged liquor into his soul, his bowels,
and he was ready to stir Sarah
to dulcet *Agony*,
so they'd fanatically stick together,
her hair scribbling over the pillows.
And then he plunged twixt her legs,
and this flooding moment bore away
all dead or dismal stars.
"Oh gosh," she moaned.

As clandestine as closeted prayer,
sleepless Miguel bade his servants ope an 8th grave:
Fresh-dug—to clasp Tobias.

Miguel suspected Tobias's death
would *immerde* he and Edna and Sarah
in national *Disgust*.
They'd be damned as *cafoni*—
as Lumpenproletarians, as rank rustics.
They'd suffer the tongues of scrupulous gossips—
that wilderness of eyes—
who deem evil words as sacred
as is *Scandal* to a tabloid.

Once the 8th grave was ready,
Miguel bade Edna to tiptoe
into the bridal *abbatoir*
to spirit Tobias's carcass—
from atop a freshly hysterical Sarah.
Then, Miguel and Edna'd lug
Tobias's grisly hulk
to the latrine-like trench,
pitch the ungodly mess therein.

Edna loathed her mission:
To again eye and sniff out a crimson-slathered mausoleum.

Miracle! Edna found the newlyweds
asleep, entwined blissfully—
languorous, languidly entangled
(like tender spaghetti).

Sarah looked even more joyous
than her ex-virgin scent did suggest;
she yielded aromas of salmon and cinnamon.

The lovers were clutching each other
as if trying to grasp each other's breaths.
Their assembly was a duet.

Once Edna told Miguel this gay circumstance,
he praised God:

"Blessed art Thou
because Thou hast *Compassion*
for two only children."

Miguel now hastened to plug Tobias's grave,
trucking sod to hide the disturbed earth:
He'd set up sunflowers gyring under the sun.

Next, Miguel asked Edna to bake challah,
and then he slaughtered 2 steers and 4 rams.

      Dawn: Tobias awoke and left his bride's bed.
Miguel kissed him and said,
"Son, tarry with us, feasting,
for 14 days,
and pleasing Sarah,
who sorely merits *Pleasure*,
given the sorrow of her 7
unsuccessful—and slain—suitors."

      Alone in her bed, Sarah awakes
and strokes her pussy—
not too much, not galore,
for, to frig oneself is to ape the devil.

      Stops she; prays she:

"I lost my breathing to gasping;
I lost my holding to grasping:
Love is a living power—
as unmanageable as *Death*."

[Roma (Italia) 6 *septembre* mmxvi]

IX

        Speedily back from his occult mission
to bind and castrate and inter[*]
the squalling eunuch, Asmodeus,
Raphael received Tobias's new commission:

"Take underlings and camels
and dispatch to Rages.
Veer to the house of Gabby
and return,
ferrying 10 sacks of long-banked silver.

        "Papa is doubtless fearing the worst,
regarding our fates.
Worry is likely festering, boiling.
To him, banjo-plucking must sound like whips, snapping!

        "Yet I cannot shorten these 2 weeks
of raucous, rambunctious shindigs—
meant to spur on fertile fucking....

        "So, do not drowse, nor tarry in shadows.
Pass swiftly through day's magnanimous, unfastened light."

        Thus, Raphael outfitted a caravan to Rages,
in Media—
to reconnoitre Gabby,
bruit Tobias's nuptials,
and pack up and trundle home Tobit's silver.

        Gabby's tourists arrived like tourists—
russet-faced at sunset.

        Twas a party bustin loose!
Music levitated like wind-borne petals!
Voices surged upward like tulips.
Trumpets flourished notes.

---

[*] *Cf. "B.T.K.": Inverse of JFK?*

Raphael now hobnobbed with Gabby,
who sat his guests to cheerful bites,
energetic gulps, stuffs magnetic to gullets.

Not too much salt on Gabby's tongue.
No vinegar in his heart.
Implacable *Hospitality*—
was Gabby's doing and giving.

Pheasant was a flush of feathers through air.
Whiskey unkinked from taps.
Among the tables, *Hooter* gals strutted,
nonchalantly short-skirted.
Damn!
In response, a cacophony of Champagne corks burst!

Night unleashed a quicksilver orchestra—
stars strumming harps of light—
until expired, emptied,
were each poet's smoking, volcanic lungs.

And after night's hematite-blackness,
light preened, promenading.

(Night blanched due to dawn's denigration.)

Now, Gabby measured out the silver—
to the letter
of lbs (or #s or £s).*

The coins shed distractin *Brilliance*—
like moths clottin bout a sizzlin candle.

---

* Cf. The Cantos, *"when Ezra had prayed, and when he had confessed, weeping and casting himself down…" (Ezra 10:1)*. Bladed narration—that's Confession—with knives set to thrust!

Thus, Raphael now collected
10 sacks of capital silver,
with 4 sacks ballasting 2 camels—
and 1 sack each weighing down the 2 servants—*

and Gabby, also astride a camel, schlepped along.

Raphael now steered the silver-backed camels
(or the camel-backed silver) home to Miguel.

Harrying dawn's vapours,
the camels floated cross sand.

Sunlight wintered, sultry around em—
as if imported from Florida.

Back at Miguel's, Raphael and Gabby
found Tobias slouched at a wine-barrel,
his mouth drooling, his pants undone.

Liquor-daggered, Tobias clambered—
staggered—into his wheelchair to go to Gabby,
and trade kisses, and cry.

"May God preserve your *Health*
unto a satisfying elderhood,
and then pass ya directly into celestial *Eternity*."

Candle light intensified
the light of *Reminiscence*
aglow in Gabby's eyes.

[Roma (Italia) 5-7 *septembre* mmxvi]

---

* *Cf. Ezra 1: 9-11 & E.P., Canto XLV.*

X

        Daily, Tobit pondered on Tobias:
How fared the boy's wandering?
His wife—Anna—feared,
"He's extinguished, exterminated, x'd."

        Weeping, daily, Anna protested her stupidity
at letting Tobias
undertake a suicidal sojourn to Gabby:

"Why didn't I distrust sty-reeking theologians?
"Too many scriptures are misspelled
or misconstrued,
allowing devils to advance evils."

        Birth is, she knew, the tripwire of *Death*;
and a map is a chessboard—
rife with pitfalls, traps, *Treachery*.

        (Yellow sunlight cheers all, aye,
but such also yellows August leaves.)

        Tobit counselled Anna:

"That man—Raphael—sounds angelic.
Expect Tobias to return."

        Tobit chastised her foreboding as "unfurthersome"
(unhelpful), as so much "astrolatry"
(star worship), and "funibrial"
(funereal) nonsense.

        Anna accused Tobit of spewing "Cat Latin"
(incoherent chatter) and "cantor's poetry"
(doggerel).
His "wisdom" was no better than "twangdillows"
(fiddle music).

"If we die childless—unchilded,
who will close our eyes, dress us for coffins?"

Anna had nightmares of a humid execution—
buttery sweat become livid blood.
She figured wolves had torn apart Tobias;
or robbers had knifed him.

Daily, Anna'd run to the doorway,
scan the road to the horizon,
seek vainly the silhouette—
or shape—of her son.

"Another day's sun gone—
My son's done gone—
Night is everyday that we're alone.

"Are his sandals tarnished?
His heart unhoused?
Is Tobias now scrunched up in a sandy hole,
Undetectable amid desert?"

The hours seemed deadly to watch.

In reality, nightly, 14 times,
Sarah the bride and Tobias the groom
had revelled in lovetoil,
never levelling off,
even come apex and acme.

Every night heard moan-gnawed air.
The newlyweds boasted gladiator passions.

At conjunction, the head of Tobias's penis
was squarely as triangular
as the valentine of his wife's vagina.

His beneficent *Efficiency*—
their hungry, mutual thrusting, snorting—
saw the lad tusking into her gaping, open flesh.

Once the 2-week-fiesta was done,
Tobias had to quit Miguel and Edna,
and, with Sarah, and Raphael, servants,
camels, and silver,
repair to his parents.

Tobias explained to his in-laws,
"I fear my folks fear me deceased."

Miguel could not bear to let his only son-in-law
take his only daughter—child—away.
He and Edna prayed to see Sarah impregnated first.

But Tobias replied, "*Hospitality* is *Tyranny*
when a guest is compelled to stay."

Miguel relented, and gifted Tobias promptly
with half of his—Miguel's—property,
including male slaves (Nubian)
and female slaves (Greek),
oxen, sheep, donkeys, camels—
silk, linen, woolens, leather—
gold coins, silver bars, and cutlery—
plus goblets, dishes, pillows, lamps—
not to mention olive oil, bread, wine, vinegar—
and sundry articles, comforts, and necessities.

Thus, Miguel and Edna bade farewell to Sarah
and her 8th husband,
but hugged both tightly,
hotly demanding grandchildren—"ASAP!"

Miguel instructed Sarah to be so virtuous a wife
as to turn gossip into eulogy.
She gotta exhibit "white-paper *Purity*."

      Edna begged Tobias to return safely
to she and Miguel
and cart along babes to satisfy their old eyes.

      Then, Edna bent Tobias to her bosom
and whispered,
"Lunge at Sarah's sex, her molten cave.
Feel her nether hairs fringing thy shaking rod;
feel your heartbeat biting through your cock veins.

Plunger in her and spend and linger,
to usher on grandchildren."

[Roma (Italia) 8 *septembre* mmxvi]

XI

      En route to Kaserin, opposite Nineveh,
Raphael tutored Tobias, "Recall how we left your father.
Let's precede well your wife and the caravan,
to announce to Tobit this blessing."

      (In truth, Raphael wants to flee generic *Peril:*
He's spied Anna's *Orgasm*-carved, death-mask grimace.

      Raphael imagines Sarah and husband,
their sexes fishing, jigging, meshing.
But the angel doesn't want to ponder
Sarah's beautiful trembling
where Tobias's nimble kisses dance limber,
or how her scalp gleams,
bobbing up from her husband's thighs.)

      Raphael instructs Tobias:
"Have the (fish) gall ready."

      As they make their way into the desert,
a bulldog traipses after the duo.
He's wary of all concealment.

      From its canine perspective,
humans daren't hide any of their reeking,
pungently fragrant acts—
of *Crime* or *Love*.

(Their parliaments are ONLY wattle, daub, dung.)

      The mutt growls,
unimpressed by Raphael's concealed—
invisible—
wings.

Anna keeps scrutinizing the Lothian Road,
squinting at the jagged horizon
to scrounge up Tobias's image.

(Each line of verse is a horizon
swamped by the pursuing line
of blanking ink.)

At last—answered prayer is apprehended:
Anna ogles her son's approach.

Outta garbled light—
what chances through the high-wall ivy—
Anna translates Tobias's aspect and figure.

Was the end imminent
of her "metromania"—
the mad recital of *Poetry*
perverted into prayer?

(Well, even wine's monotonous
until the Beloved appears.)

Anna shouts to Tobit,
"Lo! Tobias returns with loyal Raphael!"

Raphael instructs Tobias,
"Smear the fish gall on Tobit's eyes;
this medicine will repeal that gauze
that blanks out his vision."

Through whirling dust, Anna races to hug Tobias:

"Now that I've seen you,
I'm ready to die:
To see God!"

Given Anna's Passion,
she could've tumbled down as dauntless as her tears.

        Tobit creaks up from his wheelchair
and stumbles out his courtyard door.
But his movements are sloppy—
as if due to palsy, a brand of narcosis.
But, nay, he's simply been at his wine again.

        Tobias now runs to help his father, to be his crutch,
but he also hazards—instantly—
rubbing fish gall onto his father's blank eyes.

        Tobias applies gobs of gall—
like rain desperate to flood—
to his sire's eyes.

        Tobit cries out at once, "I see! I see!—
shapes, colours—if yet indistinct!"

        Now, starting at each corner,
Tobias lifts the gauze from Tobit's eyes,
and the man's 20/20 vision revives!

        The scum comes off as whitewash—
like the pale, slimy texture of *Sin*,
what streams out as pus.

        Tobit exclaims, "Thou, Tobias,
are the light gladdening my eyes!"
His eyes flash back sunlight—
as glossy as a crow.

        "Blessed be God,
Curer of *Affliction*,
Whose *Mercy* arrests *Crime*
And delivers *Benediction*."

        (*Woe* is—as domestic as rats,
as domesticating as lice.)

       Tobias relates further blessings:
"God has let me bring you a daughter—
Miguel's only daughter—
Sarah, my wife, ex-Nineveh....
Plus, servants and camels plod home,
redeeming thy silver."

       Soon, Tobias swivels in Tobit's
cherry-sweet leather, office chair.
He feels weary—as if he's traversed leagues
of *Oblivion*.
He whispers to his papa, Tobit,
murmuringly of Sarah,
his "soft-marble angel,"
a statement that makes the secret angel—
Raphael, hovering—
corrugate his brow of chocolate leather.

       Now, Tobit, freed from his wheelchair,
ecstatic, kicks it aside,
and saddles a camel—
to go to meet his daughter-in-law.

       An apocalypse of shutters!
Nineveh's Jews peep at the all-seeing Tobit.
Each window accepts an explosive push;
each shutter shunts sideways or upwards.

       When the people of Nineveh register
Tobit leaping—solo—from a camel,
and striding along, all on his lonesome,
his head gyring left and right
or periscoping up and down—
just like a man of vision—
they realize they're auditing a miracle.

Tobit's stride is as cleansing of air
as is a slap across the face.
He shouts adoration of God
and knocks aside The Commons gates
(squeaking the kinky hinges),
and treats dust and sand
to unequivocal thrashings
with each slap of his sandals.

Tobit announces proudly,
"God's restored my son, my sight, my silver,
and gifted me a mama to sire grandchildren.
There's no god like God!"

Greeting Sarah, his son's bride,
Tobit says, "Come home, daughter, with my son.
Come home, now, to blessing and *Joy*."

Tobit throws aside his cloak like a tattered blanket,
to clasp his daughter-in-law bodily,
so that she can feel his blood
drumming through his heart
while her beauty plays dramatically
to the theatre of his eyes.

All the Nineveh Jews rejoice,
yelling, "*Damn!* What fine news!"
All celebrate Sarah's elegant complexion,
that milky, crayon tint.

Tobit's household merriment runs 24/7.

[Roma (Italia) 9-10 *septembre* mmxvi
& Halifax (Nova Scotia) 16 *septembre* mmxvi]

XII

      Forks shimmied among pomegranate,
Persimmon, plums, and pears.
Once strutting, chickens dissolved to guileless bones.
Each dish was a messy success.
Gravy tasted like burnt frost.

      Once feasting abated to belching,
Tobit told Tobias, "Son, see to settling
Raphael's wages, and add a bonus."

      The oldster intoned,
"Like an ambassador from a conquered country,
Raphael has zero to say
that isn't calculated *Equanimity*;
but give Raphael his wages."

      Tobias advised: "Let's stave off
any temptation to voice political white lies.
Present Raphael half of the silver."

      Tobit responded, "Only politicians boast façades:
Raphael gets 50% of my coinage—to the letter."

      "Yep! Thanks to Raphael, father,
I have a wife; you have your eyes.

      "Note: Greenery turns to timber, to logs:
Likewise, *Marvel* becomes *Nonchalance*
and then *Boredom*.

      "For instance, a minute's silence does
in most silent reading of *Poetry*—
which sounds normally a scandalous, boisterous *Art*—
if practiced right,
unmuzzled, unmuted,
but said *loud*,
as good as its words....

So let's be loud in shouting *Praise* to God.

"(*Charity?* The elite stones are diamonds
because first they are coal.)

"If it weren't for God's intercession,
there'd be a plague of dead husbands, dead babies."

Now, Tobit summoned Raphael to his refreshed eyes,
and bade him leave the household forthwith—
with (for *Compensation*)—
50% of the silver.
"Let's say, 'Ciao.'

"And recognize:
Thou hast payouts from Miguel
and payouts from Gabby:

Silver from one
and silver from the other."

But Raphael drew Tobias and Tobit aside,
and said, "It's meet to protect a king's secrets,
but God wants, demands, open and vocal *Worship*.

"Likewise, prayer and fasting are goods,
but *Charity*—righteous—is superb.
Poverty with *Righteousness* is better than *Wealth*
got—or kept—by *Crime*.

"Likewise, we are commanded to *Honesty*.
Thus, I produce this revelation:

Tobias, while you and Sarah prayed on your wedding night,
it was I who cast out Asmodeus to Egypt,
and cut the balls off im and bound the demon,
and prisoner'd him neath the Sphinx.

"Likewise, whenever, Tobit,
you went out to shovel dirt over Hebrew cadavers,
even abandoning your honey and wine and candles,
to do so,
I was the angel who winged your deeds to God.

"And I was sent to free Sarah to cleave to Tobias
and to restore your eyes, Tobit.

I am Raphael, one of God's Angels."

The sun looked infernal gold.
Suddenly, Raphael looked an all-devouring conqueror.

The two mortals—father and son—dropped at once
to plant their faces in the earth they usually stepped over.
Stupefied, they awaited the angel's august *Judgment*.

Each man's countenance—
buried in dust, dirt, dung—
allowed breath to come only pantingly—
as a needful, desperately needed sustenance.

To their ears, the angel's speech was
a dialect of breath and heartbeats.
No: Bitter consonants.

Tobit knew he'd chisel these events
on stone tablets;
carve weighty sentences as lingering witnesses.

Raphael was an angel, but not a saint:
He'd practiced *Deceit*; he'd felt intimations of *Lust*.
He knew human weakness.

    Pityingly then, he drew Tobit and Tobias
to their feet, and said,
"Fear not! Stand!
The *Good* that I served to you was commanded
by the most High.

    "Now I ascend back to the most High.
But ask thee to scribe a scroll of these events."

    As Raphael ascended, he morphed
from dove into thrown-out crow.
He angled—dangled—in air,
then got swallowed up by the blinding sun.

    Tobit and Tobias stood, but cringed—
as if cockroaches.

    Really, all three black men gleamed—
iridescent.
But the angel was now invisible.

[Enfield (Nova Scotia) 17 *septembre* mmxvi
& Eden Mills (Ontario) 18 *septembre* mmxvi
& Ottawa (Ontario) 20 *septembre* mmxvi
& Washington (District of Columbia) 22 *septembre* mmxvi]

XIII

        Tobit prayed, "Blessed is the Eternal
who raises the saintly up—
outta abyss, crevice, grave.

        "But down go scrofulous jackasses,
bleeding assholes, shit-faced solicitors,
real-estate sluts, *les vendu(e)s*,
and necks that hazard blades—
surgery resembling a necklace.

        "The deaths of these heathens
is no worse than erasing clichés.

        "Who will not exalt God's *Majesty*?
Who will not acknowledge His authority
in—and over—Jerusalem?

        "The Divine cheers captives!

        "His blazing sunbeams sear shadows—
sterilizing, exterminating even bacteria,
and prying open tombs and prison cells.

        "Lord, thy sunlight clears, cauterizes,
venereal scabs—
eliminates all surgeries, doctors' stitches, plasters....

        "Thy sun is treasure—thriving,
and startles darkness.
The sun's hours are a journey of *Music*—
as utopian as a poem.

        "Lord, who hath copyright on Thee?
Every honest poem seeks to read Thy heart.

"Abundance? Happy redundancies!
So it is with Thou, God.
Thy red wine is red-letter liquor.
Thy scriptures are executioners' pages.
No sermon survives as counterfeit.

"To be poor, in Thine eyes, is to be rich."*
Each pink womb mints gold legacies—
good as gold coins.

"Thou freest the condemned from the gallows.
The Beloved may duck the noose
and crow Thy praises.

"Lord, the evil are desolate figures,
unmoored by *Treason*:
Power makes stiff their necks—
and then their heads go to axes.
Soon, maggots sport in their wounds—
gobbling, squirming, distilling,
snacking, drilling down to bone.

"Why don't motherfuckers heed Thee?

"Damned—immediately—are those who attempt
to curse Thy Temple—
or to tumble Thy towers.

"Privilege, instead, the faithful;
spite naysayers' pillaging tongues
and the lice-spilling lungs of persecutors.

"Sprawl foes into white space;
white em out with floods of flame.

---

* *Cf. Villon's "Panegyric to the Court of Parliament."*

      Let goliaths howl like ants
caught in termite mandibles.

      "All should heed Thee, Lord God!
The towers of Jerusalem gleam pure gold—
thanks to their 24-carat sculpting.

      "Now, all nations—the most distant—
the most estranged—hear Thy name,
and will come to Jerusalem
to shout out Thy name."

[Washington (District of Columbia) 23 *septembre* mmxvi
& Montréal (Québec) 28-29 *septembre* mmxvi
& Lunenburg (Nova Scotia) 1 *octobre* mmxvi]

XIV

  Tobit's salutations to the Most High—
and his incense
(mixing aromas of venison and cedar)
were original.

  Adoration fuelled his heart.

  Yet, he was too-soon, himself, deceased,
at 112 years of age,
and yet buried with military honours at Nineveh.

  When Tobit was settled into the earth,
it was as if he were a saint being embedded in honey.

  The priest's *Sorrow* curdled into
bittersweet, dark-chocolate words.

  Tobias's *Grief* poured out
as shaky, shivering, slop-bucket ink—
the blood of his brittle, breakable, broken heart—
i.e., ballads blue with broken English and bad words....

  Yet, Tobit had abdicated from *Trouble*,
and had favoured
the satin presence of his spouse,
Genealogy unfurling like a book.
Then, his hinge of breath closed.

  Tobit'd foreseen wounds and scars for Israel.
He'd sketched out Nahum's[*] prophecies.

  (Chalk cackles in a teacher's fingers:
It squeaks out *Equivocations*.

---

[*] *Nahum [Nattt] Shaka's.*

The clock's second-hand is second-hand dying—
the swirling, steady scythe—
like a scuttling swarm of sabres—
the whirling, steady balance—
Death and *Justice*—
measured, retardless.)

Due to their sins, Hebrews would soon bear
accentuated welts,
unquestionable welts.
An owl-masked emperor and a pig-masked general
would stack up bodies resembling *Vitiligo*—
black gangrene rotting away bleached skin.

Lineages would become bleeding amusements,
jokes of *Extermination*.

A battering ram would blast open the temple.
Next, weightless flame would desecrate the edifice,
char it to stubborn leavings—
waxy grease, fragile ash.

The temple would suffer an invincible blaze.
Shining fire would suffocate the edifice.

The people were going to be so shackled down—
so frigging shackled down!
Maculated, cut down to sulphurous *Silence*.

Amid the muffled clanking of the slave coffle,
philosophers would ponder *Liberty*.

His dying nigh, Tobit had summoned Tobias
to warn him, "Trust Nahum's prophecy for Nineveh!
So, hie thee to Media—
and get the hell outta Assyria and Babylon,
for all of Israel's gonna be shattered
even Samaria and Jerusalem—
and every Jew scattered.

"And the Temple of God at Jerusalem?
Thou will witness an orgy of souls aflame;
smoke will gallop from windows....

"As a volcano flares up from Arctic blankness,
so will fake gods face fracturing flames:
Turbulence'll tuck em in,
then *Catawumpus* unfold,
blanketing em in obscurity—
as dense as the innards of a dog's ass.

"God is as absolutist as a mirror
and as arrogant as the sun—
or a cloud.

"But these ominous archives also foretell *Redemption*.
God will rescue His people from dark *Extinction*.

"Moreover, all the backward nations will be converted—
with all idols being cast-down, destroyed,
due to their promotion of *Error*.

"Run from Nineveh! Get away!
A tidal wave of assassins[*]—
Grief become *Vengeance*—
roars down upon us!

"On whatever day you may bury your mom beside me,
do not dally even that night; leave at once!
Scram!"

Tobias did inter his mother beside Tobit.
Then, he and Sarah and children vamoosed to Ecbtana,
where Tobias died, aged 117.

---

[*] *Their breath is thorns, their garb is ice, and they love murdering.*

But before Tobias died, came dispatches
describing Nineveh's doom,
and he saw her prisoners being led
into Media,
those whom King Cyanide
had snatched and chained.

Next arrived a government
of heavy hands, heavy steps,
stifling lovers' heavy breathing.

This news—as old as soil—
is hollered from poem to poem.

How prisoners' prayers are blues;
inmates' *matins* are mother's milk mourned!

How *War* cultivates graveyards
as gardens where predators picnic!

[Lunenburg (Nova Scotia) 1 *octobre* mmxvi]

Bread, Water, Love

John B. Lee

The Elemental Is Monumental:
A contemplation of John B. Lee's
Bread, Water, Love

Despite the encrustation over millennia of very learnèd babble—Greco-Latin, German, Anglo, Hebraic, etc.—which encases biblical exposition, the text itself is resolutely elemental, organic, in its interests. Morphemes like "vomit" and "piss" decorate the homely, yet lovely (one-part Leah and one-part Rachel, so to speak) Word of God, and where one "spills seed," another is "smote"; and punishments for miscreants may include "sulphur and brimstone," while "milk and honey" may comfort the redeemed. One does not have to be a Christian or Jew or *fidèle* of any sort to recognize that biblical texts can be salty, for they are addressed to the salt of the earth, those whose tears are vinegar and whose flesh is, sooner or later, dust. Crucially, John B. Lee—The Poet Laureate of the city of Brantford in perpetuity and Poet Laureate of Norfolk County for life—is (and always has been) very aware of the dirt, gilt, breath, bread, wine, water, lungs, heart, genitals, muscles, ale, roses, weeds, dung, hosannas, and sobs that define our mortality, our pleasures and our sufferings. Reading him, one hears—properly—echoes of other spiritual poets of the elemental (a branch of the eleemosynary), especially Dylan Thomas and Thomas Merton, but also Wallace Stevens, and, to name an Anglo-Canadian poet, Al Purdy: Not that Purdy was as spiritual as is Lee, but that Lee is as elemental as Purdy.

To find the sustained, inspirited lyricism of a poet tutored in the rustic as well as the urbane, one need look no further than the third strophe of "Black Snow, Lost Light:"

and I am watching for [the vultures'] wake
to come descending in an exhilarating swoop
meant for cleaning the beach
with its rancid hunger of uncovered carrion
shrugging in the waves
rolling in the combers
lying in a tatterdemalion of bone and feathers
on the shore like half-born ghosts
gone brown in the marrow as damp branches[....]

    There is so much undiluted, unembarrassed, just frank and obvious excellence in such imagery, such rhetoric. Believable it is that this speaker has seen these predacious birds alight on a beach and havoc the offal, tearing at carcasses. Not only that—not only is Lee's speaker a kind of devotee of Audubon—but he dares to see the potential beauty of these dread creatures that "long to be lovely" as they hover over "water tarnished like neglected silver." His eye—each—is as charitable as his heart....

    It is right to focus on the elemental in Lee's work: Bread is reward for labour; and it's what is served at the Last Supper and in Victorian dungeons; ditto for water, which slakes the thirst of the prisoner and—as vinegar—becomes a wry tonic for the crucified Messiah. Yet, Lee is also a descendant of the Metaphysical poets (so beloved by T.S. "Idiot"); so abstract terms—like *Love*—are also primary to his perspective, yet secondary, still, to his impressively imagined scenes as in "The Black Hand Speaks":

... dip its phantom hand deep in the printer's hell box
full of broken vowels and fractured consonants to find there
the kind of black-fingered truth to be found only at the last
in this long apprenticeship we all of us must serve

    Lee—or maybe I should say, Johnny B. "Good"—knows that the soul can only be saved as it is manifested in the living body—

the corps before it becomes a corpse. Nor is *Love* incarnate save where bodies can have and hold one another (and reproduce)—spiting the doom that's our mortality:

go build me
a darkness large enough
to hold
the cave of stars
and give me the torch
of a smouldering mind
I will smudge
the walls
with a blackening stick
where beasts
leap to life in the sky

That last quotation from late in the book presents the speaker as *maker*, weaving constellations out of stars just as cave men—and women—imagined their quarry as captured spirits. Thus, we learn that *Art* is holy—*Loving*—magic; the elemental rendered monumental.

George Elliott Clarke
Poet Laureate of Toronto (2012-15)
Parliamentary Poet Laureate (2016-17)

Bread, Water, Love

*I dedicate these poems to
my wife Cathy*

"*First you shall have bread; then you shall have water*"
an ancient Hittite quotation translated from cuneiform

Preface

The poems in *Bread Water Love* were written in a lake house on a cliff overlooking Long Point Bay in Port Dover, a commercial fishing port, located on the south coast of Lake Erie. The title for this collection involves the conflation of a Hittite phrase deciphered from Cuneiform and the words of a Hittite king who was the first member of a royal family to use the word 'love' in a poem dedicated to his wife.

When I was an adolescent studying ancient history in grade twelve, I became fascinated with the Hittites who also appeared in the Old Testament. Having been reminded of that younger self, I watched a documentary on Hittite civilization and it was there that I learned of the ancient Cuneiform text quoted here and of the love of the Hittite king for his wife. Although the poems herein have little to do with the Hittites, the themes of bread, water, love figure as an inspiration for the poems.

I am reminded also of Omar Khayyam's famous lines:

A book of verses underneath the bough,
A jug of wine, a loaf of bread—and thou
Beside me singing in the wilderness—
O, wilderness were paradise enow!

John B. Lee

Poems from Bread, Water, Love have appeared in Adam, Eve, & The Riders of the Apocalypse anthology, Michigan State University Poet Laureate anthology, Transitory Tango anthology, The Ambassador: Volume 014, Literary Connection, Volume 2, Suffering the Intelligence of Love: In Light and in Darkness anthology, Voices Israel, Quills, The Literary Gourmet Re-visited and Verse Afire. A few of the poems have been translated into Spanish by Manuel Velázquez León. The poem 'Black Snow, Lost Light,' won Honourable Mention in the Spring Pulse Poetry Competition and was published in the journal commemorating that event, and the title poem 'Bread, Water, Love' has been set to music and recorded by Michael Schatte for his latest CD.

Bread, Water, Love

"Now you will eat bread,
  Further you will drink water."
    a Hittite phrase deciphered from Cuneiform

four thousand years ago
in a warm embrace of words

bread, water, love
if I lie
in the living arms
of language
what better words
than those—
bread, water, love
to give our common sleep
of dust
a gift of breath

bread

       water

              love

Here in the Day

we must
enter the house
by the door in the wall
or the window
open to the wind
but I am all
for floating in
as the shadow
falls to the well
or light on water goes deep
with the sharp and silver knife
of the sun
as it wafts through linen or
as the green leaf also warms
the root

here in the day you have the brick
and mortar moment
with disappearing underside
and the mason's law for monument
the heavy hod's grown light
with its rope less taut
the hardened lime that shapes
a line of grey to greet the clay
within the clay

the gecko clings and rushes up
to empty blue
and the common mouse
has pantry drawers to gnaw
as with an essing tail
to vanish
through the dream gap
of a scurry hole
where darkness grows most dark
and time in life's
like something candle-poked
some soft surmise
of fire melt
and smoky breath
the leaning flame
blinks like a word
we've said in air
for wishing when the wax is sweet
and then and there the mouth
takes in the field

Unmistakable Strangers

all winter
my wife has been feeding
the wild creatures that live in the town
mostly sparrows
singing in the grain
the odd
exotic red-capped woodpecker, dark-eyed junkos
cardinals, blue jays, common starlings, grackles
the yellow flash of a finch
and interloping rodents
chipmunks, rabbits and
from among a plentitude
of squirrels one particularly fat princely squirrel
sleek-furred and friendly—comes
to the window in the morning
along with the early light
demanding the same attention
his tail high
and throbbing its flag
for want of food
her favourite, she
falls in love
like a waitress at a diner
with an ever-returning customer
who comes to the counter
every day
for small talk, a smile
and an oven-warm wedge of homemade pie

this squirrel
no longer anonymous
an unmistakable stranger
from the nameless throng
of this dog-worried neighbourhood
walks the railing
and peers in
on self-reflected longing

when spring blossomed
and cold-nosed snow
shrank to a blink
like wet paper gone water-grey in the gravel drive
the crows called down
to the carrion in the street
at the front of the house
and the vultures
dropped black-winged shadows
on the beach at the back
crows
plucking away at the jawline
of life
vultures celebrating death
with its voluminous appetite
standing shoulder to shoulder
at the lake's edge

Songs for a Bountiful Solitude

a solitary ring necked drake
floats alone
on the cold waves
of a Lake Erie winter
diving under fishing grey-water shallows
near the shore
by the shale-rubble pier
where I also live
a poet's life
knowing there is one moon of the night
one star in the day
as it is with one black-bodied hunger
riding the bountiful surf
of invisible life
he vanishes and seems
to drown
like the drawn-under voices
of those lost forever
in storms of the past
with whom the morbid nets of this town
are overfull
like the veil
that catches a widow's breath
as she sobs
to say her husband's name
as it empties itself on a stone

this is the lonesome work
we do
we who dive
through vacant deeps
with a word
for the fish and the ghost
of the fish
those that school in a dream   unseen

Black Snow, Lost Light

i

my little dog
takes offense–yapping up
at the kettle of vultures
hovering in ovals of flight over his yard
and it's not as though they were in search
of lost light or late-winter death
riding the thermals
seeming to take pleasure in ethereal movement
catching the blue perfection
of an uncommonly warm March afternoon

they are looking down on their own angelic forms
tracing burn-shadows drifting over the earth
their naked faces ugly and red raw as the inner flesh
of a recent wound

and I am watching the lake ash
for their volt
and I am watching for their wake
to come descending in an exhilarating swoop
meant for cleaning the beach
with its rancid hunger of uncovered carrion
shrugging in the waves
rolling in the combers
lying in a tatterdemalion of bone and feathers
on the shore like half-born ghosts
gone brown in the marrow as damp branches
and what is this that discontinues
along with black snow melting backwards
ice rotting with a feral hiss as it vanishes

into steel-coloured wash
the face of the water tarnished like neglected silver
or the flecked surface of antique-shop mirrors
smearing reflection and ruffing a foamy collar
for the jutting shale not quite Shakespearean enough
for serious contemplation of the grave, but sad nonetheless
and these vultures long to be lovely
even with their appetite for sorrow in the squirrel house
sorrow in the carp school
and the insatiable gloominess of the truth of dying

ii

a lone robin
its red breast etiolated
by late spring gloaming
when what is rust-red blackens
with unreflected light
and there he stands
perched high
on a bent twig
his body sleek with hunger
wing-tucked and singing
for his solitary want of the ear's attention
and it is going-on-toward Easter
when the altars
will be draped
and the candles snuffed
on this day of remembering fog-in-the-morning
come in veils trailing over the lake
like the ghost brides of lost sailors
and the land lifts and is smouldering with frost loss
like the last heat from buried fire
and I am reminded
of how my pulse quickens
in this newly lonesome cold
and I am become the robin
wanting to be someone else's last thought
before sleeping
when the sky draws down
on aging daylight

Cursing Underwater

"All in whose nostrils was the breath of life,
of all that was in the dry land died."
Genesis 7, 22

if I taste the painted apple
with the knowledge
of my tongue
it comes away in silken oil
and crimson linen or
something buttered smooth on
woven hemp, and who am I to blame
the chemical flavour
of linseed and cinnabar for
confabulated branches
on imaginary grafts
what pulls me under
rises up
like gravity and loft

the buoyant feather
and the stonework wall

what's weed-wave green
and white-star blind
is cursing underwater
though that outrage will not cure the drowned

why bless the fishes
with the flood, Lord
the shark has his advantage
his black eye blinks
in supersaturated salt
to wonder
at the grace of being
given gills
he might rend the bloated moral
of bad weather
with a double tooth
so sharp it tears the rainbow twice

oh mine is like the sorrow of a sunken jug
so deep it lets the darkness go
one word to break the surface, one word to close the wound
one word to lift the yellow ointment of a water soothing moon

The Gift

you have given me the gift
of a beautifully spackled stone
the size and shape
of a baker's loaf of hard bread
you say you brought it among many
to your own porch labouring home
from the Leslie Street Spit   east side
carried it as heavy leaven
a yeasty lapidary monument
round-heeled and weather-worn
brought as ballast
perhaps from Dorinish Island
off the Irish coast
where grain ships
harvested rock for the empty hold
crossing vast grey waters
for want of Canadian wheat
and why is it
that there in window light
on the oaken rail
of my parlour ledge
along with carved goose
and whelk shell and wood loon
and lighthouse lamp
as I think also
of the green-bearded lake stones
waving weed life in shore wash
like the fringed skulls of the drowned

and I know
by the ghost and soul
of lost fog
what thrives in granite
and shale
and in the great still heart
of a hill and in the fossil's thumb-worried womb
where Selkies dream
in luminous shadows of a bay-lit moon

Not Nothing

what begins in the hard-shelled seed
has this strange packed-in result
thrust for show on its stalk going up and into the rafters
of the fair barn
the heavy-headed droop
of the dark-faced corolla
the lonesome and most tall
helianthus of the sunflower field
the freakish giant looking down
its petals blackened by time
as it is also
with ditch weeds
and roses
and every other autumnal ripening

as with the lazy pluck
of unattended sorrow
everything ages to this and also
the big-bellied gourd nearby
placed on a board - the corpulent orange-rind fellow
with an insatiable appetite, a singular gluttony
for sun and shade and earth and water
and the sick-skinned
injection of growth-inducing drugs

what a hollowing out by time
entering into the wine and cider rot
of abandoned orchards
with the brown sloven
of all over-ripening red
like light
that fades through crimson smoke
at sundown
that big blush of beautiful heaven falling west through blue
at day's end

and then I stand
at the intersection
of Grand Boulevard and
Lawton Avenue
in old Detroit
bend down and gather back
one broken brick
fallen to the sidewalk
from the ruin
of the Lee Plaza
the honeymoon hotel
where my father first took
my mother
in his loving arms
like David his Bathsheba

gone the terracotta lions
gone the copper roof
gone the American walnut panels
gone the bronze doors
gone the Peacock alley and plush room luxury
of individual suites
gone the glass to black
gone every opulent thing
replaced by razor wire
frost fence and low-grade graffiti

my son
shows me a photograph
he's taken
of a bead of water
on an upcurled green leaf
and within that
droplet jeweled with light
a small creature seems to blink
like the music of Motown
a young boy in Beatle boots
clicking backwards along Woodward Avenue
vanishing into the womb
like a winter apple into the earth beneath
an all-forgetting purity of stone-cold snow

The Sculpture

we speak of the beauty of the female form
as we regard
the bronze sculpture
of a young woman
her body burnished
in lamplight of the living room
of your mother's apartment
and you tell us
how you, her son, were the artist's assistant
transforming her plaster cast
with scalded wax
and the patina
of chemical washes
with the almost visible brush strokes
of the mind
following the soft lines
of the belly
down the long form
of her thighs
to the lovely instep
of the intimate soles
of her feet at rest
as though we were all there
in the Master's hands
at the last moment of Adam's lonesome
and solitary sleeping

this being
the divine need
of all creation—what's
overlooked by incompletion
where in the gentle rub
of sensual shapes
from the rounding
to the fold we are incarnate
with the milk weep of wanting
that seeps from mammalian design
the rasping away
of the seam lines
those creased erratum of the mold

and we all shine
like apples in sunlight
even the windfalls
even the bruised and teeth-broken
weather-scattered cider stink
and rot-away of unattended autumns
we who are life-proven
and given over
to the worshipful caress
of memory and dream
and the sacralizing reverence of a lover's
loving touch

The Red Tailed Hawk

we sat in conversation on the hill
when the red tailed hawk
arrived
hovering in the updraft
rising off the lake
her body arched
wide wings shivering to keep her still
talons set
keen eye fixed
sharp beak bent
in concentration
on some movement
in the tangled gorse
the golden rod, the crown vetch
the thistle gone to seed
green-shadowed vole
beware, wee mouse be quiet
walleyed doe
twitch your whiskers in the knowing dust
and wait
the time to hold your breath
is now
amazement plucks its fly-jeweled web
like angels of a silent harp
see how she stays the course
as though a dab of solitary brown gone dry
within a blue-brushed work of art
and if
what breaks a rodent mother's quickening heart
weren't real
the thrill that carves the nostril

rends to rags all hope of sparrow feel
the raptor in design
completes the argument of paradise
and shocks the sentimental dreamer from
a pleasant sleep with frantic swaths of red

Willow-want

I am struck dumb
by the incredible lightness of birds
watching the seemingly weightless
red winged blackbird
land on the high thin
branch of the willow
weeping over the lake
its small claw feet
curling
like fine wire of watchworks
the red dash of its wingfeathers
like crimson beadwork
woven into the ultra black radiance of night
and the catkin
barely responds
like breath on thread
it simply bobs
as it falls into beauty
as though the tree
were sleep dreaming
in self-caressing blue

the hollow-boned bird
come to rest
on the drop and lift
of a waterfallen green
an equally buoyant
respsonding
this ephemeral symbiosis
to see how the tree
desires the sky
with its burden of leaves

and branches
catching the aviary raindrop
of a single shadowy lamentation, life
receiving its prayer and solace
like breath on flame
that clings to the wick as it carries the smoke
the body might also likewise
cling to a thought
this bird rising as I witness
the after-wishing of an emptying upward
of willow-want   abiding

Nothing But Light

There is nothing but light shining
from the surface
of the forest pond
its cold tea-coloured water
like the tannins
of my grandmother's words
recalling her father's
late-night importuning
of her mother
saying leave the tea
in the pot
for later ...
and I imagine
steeped black liquid
kissing the gilded rim
of his delicate cup
at a starlit hour
pouring out over all
on the Mull Crossing farm
with its flatlands
masking the flesh of the dead
where frost heaved stones
rise from fields
like the froth of money from tea

and I stand here
at the trail's edge
watching where faceless moss
greens luminous water
with the wintering deadfalls
leaning along with all other
sky spilled after-silences

knowing I dare not step there
as though upon tension
with its moody rumour
of mud tracked by a ghost in the house

but oh—if I were a child
what a splashing I'd do
gone to the ankle
gone to the hip
gone to tips of my hair
waving in the shallow deeps
like bottom weed
where reflection is real
and where everyone weeps
to be found

Still Warm and Burning

it is twenty days shy of Christmas
and a duck blind
floats offshore
in a stone-grey world
at midday
with two hunters concealed
in the tattered grasses
of that anchored island
their gun muzzles
visible from the beach
like a matched pair of smokeless chimneys
poking out of that ragged weed-black boat
riding the undulations of low water
that is the colour of washed away ashes
in afternoon overcast
with our own and only
most lonesome star
festering in the suppuration
of light-wounded heaven

and they wait
as though they were lingering
deep within the darkness
in the cold grotto of a fireless hill
and they are atavistic remnants
of old death bringers
as we are all made from the same
heartbeaten dust

the soul of the mallard
both drake and hen
is building one nest in the mind of the wind
as I see them scissoring over the gloom of the bay
into echoless booms
lifting from cordite puffs like lost thunder
what drops them down to the cold appetite
of that lifeless archipelago of hand-carved decoys
also lifts a long pole
with its weight of wet feathers soaked through
like something cracked at the seams
and left in damp weather
with a fire still warm at the centre still burning

The Experiment

... it has been proven by science
that if you
show someone a film
of human hands
being thrust to the wrist
in a bowl of ice
that the fingers of the viewer
will drop in temperature
by as much as two degrees ...

what then
of the vicarious chill
of the lake in darkness
how might
my heart rejoice
where the wilderness thirsts
at the sharp edge
of hard water
while the foaming surface shivers
to climb the new far shore
like a wave-exhausted swimmer
there is such a mournful wintering
by creatures of moonlight
when the nocturne howls in the flesh
and the soul responds
like looking down
from a great height
through a glass floor
and feeling
the strings of the sky

grow tight
as you float on star silk
and are wing-shouldered
angelic marionette
buoyed in the updraft of primordial dreaming

I Watch the Lake
on Morning's Christmas Eve

I watch the lake on morning's Christmas Eve
and see the white crests
of a thousand-thousand waves
become the curling under
of the blurring wings and shoulders
of a multitude of angels drowning
as they fall and sink and rise again and thrash
upon the foaming motion
as they fail the sky

last night
the sudden sorrow of a tempest
tore its water garments in a wind
that woke this house to hear
a sob of apples lately snapping on their stems
like winter auguries of withering things

an old man loves his manhood overmuch
to even in this moribund confusion
climb beside the tree
the broken ladder with its missing rungs
to feel that empty clutch of air
that vacant strut—the one the shadow climbs
to shape the horse count of the highest branch
the dizzy graft within an itch of altitude
above my reach where blue breath frames the light
as though to hold the lassitude of ghosts
when time's direction dreams a footfall
in the stars, and reaching down
confirms abundance in a broken cask of cloud

Oh, Gentle Me

I am wading into the green
weed of the cliff waist deep
in the bunch gall of the goldenrod
I'm scything nettles falling in my wake
I'm culling the big-leafed burdock
before it dare become
the dog's bane of cocklebur
thickening my terrier's coat
and snagging his tail in autumn
wagging a brown tangle
like cotted wool stained by sheep water
when I hear
something squeaking underfoot
sounding like rusted spring coils
of a rain-weathered chesterfield
under a shifting sleeper
I move away rapid
ginger-foot, spooked by the noise
of living earth
to them I am
the clumsy galumphing of unwanted intrusion
to them
I am the weighty death-shadow
of an ogrous sky

I come down glowering
like washout, I come down
like tree rot
and the broken shade of a big wind
to them
I am the dark angel
of crush and destruction
far worse than fire
I crack no pine seed open
I am the quintessential plod
of a purposeless juggernaut dancing away
like deep ice
as I carry the hill
backwards and slow
estuary slow with the small erosion
of delicate-boned mouse beauty
the impossible vole
the blind-shouldered star-nosed mole
the little crack-ribbed things
that simply
walking their way
might dispatch
all the wee children
conceived by ground-sparrow contemplation
during the songs of dawn or sunfall
breaking its blood-spotted albumin
on the crimson-shelled shrug of a blue longitude

but me–I'm afraid
what might
climb my shoe
with delicate rat-hands
white as potato sprouts growing in the night
gripping on thrill
inside my trouser-seam cuff to knee
with a whip-tail tracing its shiver
like a stripped vein
my heart quickens
at the thought
of a pointy-faced creature
greeting my manhood
like the teasing there
of an unwanted hand

oh–I'll kill and I'll
kill as
thunder kills a
big old dog
quivering into the finality of a black-hearted storm

what's this loving man
to do
bring his sharp-voiced
fear to the broken-stemmed
sweet William of the world
I am that accidental fragrance
of every unexpected
event
bringing my own worst behaviour
to bear on this occasion

please–someone scream at me
I am desperate to undo
to stop being so ineluctably human
even my soul
like smoke from struck burning
is gulping–No!

He Only Does That
When He's Thirsty for Danger

he walks Danny the dog
down the long lane through the park
to where the lake roars
and rises
over the rocks
which form a recent
breakwall of grey rubble
built to withstand wild weather
where the waves shatter
in glassy splinters
with winter ice
dashing its jagged frazil
splintering skyward like a chandelier
come whirling out of cold rage
and the big pup
an English bull mastiff
runs slobbering up out of the ditch
and over the path
tossing saliva over his own wet shoulders
which are foamy as stones in the sea
and his hind legs
push his big body sideways
so he's cantilevered like a broken machine

what is he
but wonky and lovably dumb

and my son sees
him go down over the rise
in a brown tumble
like something dumped wrong
some brick load of dog stumble
and he knows
the full result
for Danny has gone snap-branched
into the blue scramble beyond the last bolder

my son jokes later
having had to dare
the freezing combers
in an effort to rescue the fallen
braving past the grey stones
skinned in ice
at the edge of the world

and for all of the paleolimnology
lost in those old rocks
wearing time in the crack lines
and fissures
there is no lessoning for the fossils
as moths drawn to that love
flickering in ancient firelight
for a man who loves his dog
has the smouldering wings of a burning angel
and we are beautiful stupid

What Awaits Me in the Sandwash

when waves wash in
erasing every evidence of my having
gone this way, walking
west along the strand
my footfalls plush
like palms that warm cool glass
ephemeral as morning fog
this memory of mist is me
and yet
impossibly the earth
awaits my shadow strides
like branches used
to brush a dusty floor
where snakes
came essing in the night
go grip a crooked rope
to see how long
the knots will hold their truth
like dancer's distance
where the spirit keeps
its catholic heat   the heart
gone blushing down the bones
like rain within the limbs
that drink the darkness from the light

the last unlasting step
involves   unvanishing
like something taking flight
then falling upward
evaporate as stone
or like the wind caught leaf aloft
see there
I rise to wasn't where I was
and am not yet   elsewhere
the sleeper's mirror
keeps my list
and memory in other minds than mine
laments the absent presence
of my being   here and gone

The Black Hand Speaks

in among the shorn weeds on the lake cliff
my little dog goes foraging
and there he finds
for his very own canine delectation
every delicious lump of frozen cat turd
which he gobbles down quick quick
with a seemingly insatiable gluttony
like Pip's fat Uncle Pumblechook
and ever unsatisfied
he goes off
questing after
bird beak, stinking scraps of rancid hide   a lonesome fish jaw
the latter he finds lying in rubble
like a mostly rusted away crosscut
I see it picked up and pricking from his snout
his face fanged and sharp like the fractured snarl
of a northern pike - he
carries this final intention - this verdict
for swallowing hard what might hurt him

and so my little dog goes
grazing the hill
with his ravenous appetite for trash
and I wish this wish, in this wish for writing true and well
if only this poem
might dip its phantom hand deep in the printer's hell box
full of broken vowels and fractured consonants to find there
the kind of black-fingered truth to be found only at the last
in this long apprenticeship we all of us must serve

Beyond the last sandbar

beyond the last sandbar
a small regatta of gulls
float at rest
and they are shell-white
drifting in a barely seeable circle
of windless motion
each gull like a nun's cornette
if a nun were a doll
and the doll were drowned
riding the slow inbreath of resting water
rising and falling to follow old
rhythms of a sleepy measure
in calm dreaming
without foam
where the sky lay fallen
like the lassitude of blue silk settling
drawn on the loom at the hem
by a delicate tugging of a thread-sure hand

and there
to the east
a grey-black armada of Canada geese
wild waterfowl
blinking their webbed feet
coming in and going thence
to groom the beach
with the dropshadow of their reflections
like ash on water
washing away the fire
built overclose to the finality of waves
in the hissing of dampened heat
that flares up and is banked for last burning

overhead
a kettle of vultures
catch thermals
along the black drag of a ragged coast

as a sudden hawk glides through
worried by crows
chased by that caw going west
to the general rumours of awe

what is it then I wonder
to live in the wind
what is it to be born
in the rough nest
of the aerie
like a storm-broken
orchard
the oriole's pouch
the martin's motel
to thrive in the swamp
or live on the high ledge
overlooking the city

I've seen those chevrons
pulling the dark remainder of day
as it cools
and they're quickening home
to the close at hand shallows
of gloom

it is sweet to remember
and lovely to know
how the forest forgets and the forest recalls
as we enter the earth
like the rain

Sunset in Dover, September 15, 2016

I was walking west with my dog
west where the sun sank in the sky
trailing its silk
like the grand banners of a medieval army
burning blue, crimson, pink
on the silvery breastplate of evening
my wife had sent me out
in my postprandial fatigue, my ache
against movement, a grumble of bones
and the slow pull of rising
like a workhorse roped to lodged stone
and yet, for love I go
it's her love of me that sends me out
into the purity of light
and she intends to do the dishes
while I'm gone
but the lure of beauty draws her through the window
to follow
and seek me on my path
so we might share the glory
of this one particular and most spectacular
sundown, but I turn
off Greenock and Mergyl
and she misses my going
as now
the full moon blazes in the east
a sea-pocked white
that gathers my attention
into the hazy nimbus of reflected radiance

and so she retraces her steps
as she fails to have found me
at this moment
when the great broad greying of gloaming
steals divine fire
this oldest of all ideas
at the going down of inerternal day

with the dinner plates dripping in the drainer
and our sweet individual solitudes
crossing and recrossing it seems
we are shadow-lost
like the dipping of smoke from lit tallow
we smolder in the word-gift
of a good marriage, but oh with the stars of promise
we're given the gift of dreaming

The Awakening

one summer
we were children, the next
we were not
and as I stood
on the muddy bottom
of the rib-deep river
feeling the oozy marl
of the mucky bed
taking the shape of my toes
in the wet seep
of my instep
like a sculptor's thumb
in come-to-life clay
I watched
the slow descent
of bodies
coming down the dock ladder
to wade
in the liquefied blue
of a fluvial moment of flowing light

nearby the brave swimmers
dove and plunged
and broke the glass
where reflected sky shattered
and closed
above their pulled-under heels
in a sudden
and shuddering gulp
as they disappeared and
reappeared as though

through the adoration of two invisible doors
like some hooked-by-heaven
fish fighting a beautiful beam of silken air

and as I stood there
watching the wet-to-the-knee
hesitation of those at the second last rung
coming down from the tar-fragrant pier
I anticipate
an intimate lift of boat wake
from long-line Lakers
making their heavy churn
so the river rises
to stir a rope-circle of buoys
afloat at the edge
of deep water responding
like catching your breath from slaking your thirst
at the rim of a well

Eros

last night
in unlasting darkness
I walked the beach
looking up at wonder
with those grown-old galaxies
moth-winged
by the drifting veil
of an overcast

that vaporous meditation
of water's gossamer caress
also occurring within the boundary lines
of the body where
the heart beats, the soul
silkens, the mind
mulls—and the deep-shadow spirits
of lost evening must vanish to be real
like the blinking awake
of a dreamer

as though I were suddenly
unsleeping
with my memory
of the story of ancient illumination
forever recursive with its sliver of moonlight
in the corona
that cups the mist
as blind heaven comes clear
in transformation
as it is with frost grown warm
in a cooling palm

Darling, may I touch your pinkletink

in those early years of marriage
when we walked the back lane
forming the long island of meander
leading through the spring swale
surrounding us behind the house
where thimbleberries ripened through the fence
pressing crushed areolas of small fruit brambled
on the full bosom of the wet fields of Somerset
and as we strolled we heard
from both before and aft
the thrilled chorus of the swamp
singing among the red branches
of dogwood piercing the stillness
both lace and leaf
like the life of the heart throbbing
through a green mirror of algae
and something comes true—so eventual
it might
winter in us
like blush on the cheek
coming in from the cold

and I am remembered of
the quick black pollywog
pulsing in a jar
in the dill-coloured water
we stole from the pond
at school

and what it was it also seemed
flooding the world
in verdant release after my son's epithalamium
watching a swan's breast
advancing through High Park
its white reflection chasing feather-form
within the gentle chevron
of a wave's result
that proof of going towards forever
as it is with
where the hand goes
plunging in to release the stopper
in a warm bath
for the soapy clock-wind whirling
to a lovely gurgle in the gullet of a thirsty drain

we were the especial silence
at the centre
of all that singing
and it mattered not
how quietly we went

there was this secret knowledge
even of our shadow presence
even of the lucid darkness
within the limpid veil
of the least movement of the light
we were overheard by the grey caress
of bullfrogs listening
as though
to be caught singing were a sin

as the farm dog Tip
asleep in the cool
dip of the earth in the forsythia shade
of the veranda remains in the mind
long after he's under the grass

and I'm crooning on the porch
full voiced and unembarrassed
when my uncle says
"what the hell
are you doing ..."

and I know it's not a question
but an accusation

Were I

were I to meet you
in your plastic shoes
and you me
in my cowboy boots
when we were both
small in the rain
lost among all that it meant
to be
casting short shadows
with new minds
when our mothers were young
and our fathers
were shaving their dreams
in the soap scent
of long ago morning
rinsing their razors in time before time
would we have
loved the other
me in my worn-down heels
the sugar-foot lad
and you
the princess with painted toes
shining up from the floor
like chips of broken glass

oh we were playing at promise
I on my cockhorse
in the orchard
on the farm
my hat a ten-gallon green

and you in your pinafore
undressing and dressing your dolls
like the come and go
of the sea
to a darkening stone that lies
high on the shale of the shore

when you were a girl
your umbilical beautiful ultra white tummy
with its feminine lip and rim
like a green pomegranate
impossibly perfect with seed
desire abiding in sunlit
mirrors of the ribbon watered moon
and I a boy
with my whip-tailed
star dazzled want
like ghost galaxies
glazing the milk spill of night
the voluminous smear at the swirling edge
of mammalian chaos

what's cervical mucus of the spirit
what's ovum-mystical life

you in the city and
I on the farm
we awaited love's knowledge unborn

Open

open your eyes, open your heart
open your mind, open your arms
open your thighs, open your infolding flesh
involve me there
within that flowering
as though you were a butterfly in gauze
a garden in the sun
or loamy earth
beneath the muddy fragrance of the rain
and I will enter
blue rivers of desire
life pulsing round each thirsting root
one season lived in solitude
three seasons   lived alone

I am content to be contained
like pebbles plunging in the circular rhythms
of a radiant pool within the secret sorrows
of your solitary soul

When My Beloved Writes of Her Soul

when my beloved writes of her soul
in the lonesome and almost
solitary poem of her life
I am amazed also
by thoughts of her body's
beautiful design
consider the heart's work
its deep-in-the-breast abide
or the gentle machinery
of her most delicate bones
and the blue-veined wonder
of sanguinary rivers of the flesh
tracing soft light as it returns
to where she is
blushing arterial red, I too
believe in the hyper-sternal notch
or the kneecap, or the ankle
or the palm's longest line
even every small scar
even the kundalini
at the base of the spine
even the spiritual fragrance
like the bitter-sweet perfume of apple sap
weeping into green earth, I've seen
milk of the soul so white
it pours its pure perfection
like the gloss of watered silk
on the surface of the night
with its surety of stars
and the moonlit menses of our human seas

we've winter's seasons to consider
what it means to dream
a thousand sleeps
from voluble moments to
the silent seeking of a quiet grace
this my dumb journey
with its frequency of awe
I am your fortunate companion
I bend my borrowed brow
above this living page
and list my doubtful doubts
like seeds that germinate from fire
to lift green voices out of watered clay

Last Evening

we sat on the hill
overlooking the bay
and watched, keeping vigil
for the full promise
of a total lunar eclipse
the first of its kind in over thirty years
and we were anticipating how the moon
would vanish, darkening down
like the slow sliding over
of an optic lens
blurring the white circle
turning it blood orange
as it is with the fade of lamp glow
burning through gossamer autumn scrim
but here it was
a night of overcast
only a black-veiled widow visage
of reflected light visibly
piercing thin weather
blazing brilliant
through cloud gap
and then gone ghostly grey in vaporous
sweeps of wet web
we lost all hope of stars
in that gothic regard
for we were shrinking down to nothing
but a tree and a dog
and a man and a woman
seated together
in a pair of fan-backed Adirondack chairs
listening to willow whisper of a close at hand breeze
and the loud hush of the lake waves churning

On the Occasion
of the Night
of the Last Snow Moon

February 11, 2017

on the occasion of the night
of the last snow moon
we were sleeping
in the forgetful hunger
of a winter month
our bodies
obedient to dream
as we lie
under the invisible green
burning ice
of an unseen comet
going cold and close
as the trace of light
on a frost-heaved stone

go build me
a darkness large enough
to hold
the cave of stars
and give me the torch
of a smouldering mind
I will smudge
the walls
with a blackening stick
where beasts
leap to life in the sky

Driving Home at Sundown

yesterday at sundown
we were slinking west
blinded by brilliance
in the great slow
dragon of Toronto traffic
slithering over the shiny surface
of the paved river of effluvial earth
as one body we
eased toward the great cave mouth
of phosphorescent heaven's
sun-washed silver eye
slipping like some ultra-luminous
illusion of the whereabouts of light
when light has lost its purpose
in magnified retinal burn
and though we cannot see
we move
by common faith
a single-minded multitude of steel and glass
one flash
of something serpentine of mind

the watchwind of that quarter hour
with its vivid invisibility
an iridescent washing away
of material things
the rapturous road's edge—gone
the city vanishing in a lusciferace glare
of brilliant buildings
too brilliant to be seen
the radiant glass
all autoluminescent

rumours of other automobiles
the chromium shimmer of bumpers and trunks
a vivid absence of individual things

imagine the glittering spine
of a creature
shimmery wet and lashing through dazzle
... is it fear that we feel
striking its match
in the brain
of each driver
believing she is loved
or that he
is cosseted like a walking candle
lit and flickering
cupped against darkness
in the votary palm of his mother
fragrant with kitchens of home

yet little girls
drown in linseed harvest
smothering down
to a blink in the grain
and little boys
drown in the sea
in the great blue thought
of the beautifully bountiful sea

Oh, my dark companion ...

my sister tells me the story
of how
when she was a girl
she witnessed the arrival
at the girls' door of SS No 6
the village elementary school
we attended as children
and she and her friends
watched as Miss Myrtle Downie
walked up to unlock the building
as was her morning practice
and there
sheathed over the handle
some local wag
had affixed an unused prophylactic
skinning the knob
like a blister on brass
and she peeled the latex
as an audience giggled shyly behind their hands
placed the safe to her lips
and inflated the thing
as though she were about to amaze them all
with a poodle balloon
and I thought as the tale unfolded
how some rough-living prankster
some nearly-shaving rogue
some going-on-for-sixteen quitter
might have been there
secreted nearby and hiding behind
one of the pump-pump pole away maples
those tag-and-your it trees
that framed our play

where we stood in captivity
holding each other hand to hand
like a string of paper dolls

I almost hear
the stifling of raw laughter
red-faced and mean-spirited
guffaws like an old man coughing

and our schoolmarm placed
the filmy inflation
taking in a last big breath
like final wishes
as the milk-film translucence of that small zeppelin
filled her hands
and I cherish the charm of the virgin
the life-long chastity
of that dear woman
for whom we were all of us
her beloved children – every one
and I do not laugh
but smile

if I think
how last evening
in a poets' circle
we talked of Sir William Osler
that nineteenth century physician
who encouraged his medical students to pursue
a clear mind and
a loving heart
he who first saw
animalcules flowering on filmy glass
he who studied cadavers in the dead house

within the courtyard of the Blockley gardens
alive with yellow daffodils
in the Cotswold village
beside the pond
where the bronze statue of a young girl
pours out unceasing waters
from giving jug to
ever-receiving rippling pool

and if there is life eternal
in Osler's ashes
at old McGill
where all the equanimities
of one soul
radiate like the bell
we once heard
sounding over the land of our youth
calling us to attend
and give
obeisance to lost memory
as all learning is quintessential recall
of the already known

is it little wonder then
that I give Christ's benefit
to the lascivious and seemingly snide youth
hiding in the shadows of time
like everyone's dark companion

Erie Farne

*an epithalamium composed for Mary Margaret and Jonda
on the occasion of their marriage
Saturday, January 7th, 2017*

you who have built your house facing south
framed it firm on the cliff by the lake
overlooking the bay
set two lives for love in four seasons of love
keeping watch on the water
where the great boats moor
in the lee of the land
when high winds come
shaking the shore

and you've marked with your minds
where the bald eagle soars
flying west as it comes to its aerie, comes to its rest
with its perch in the willow's repose
and you guard how the paper wasp
works on its hive and has hung its grey nest
in a tree

oh the fox
with the flag of its tail
rises over the crest like a flame in the air
and this is also the hawk
and this for the hare
and these are the songs of the earth
taking wing
in the voice of those wings
working low as the geese will come low
going home

and here where the monarchs feed
their hungering orange
here where the mayflies
smoulder at dusk
as spring perfumes the lilac's breath and the blossoming crab
and summer blooms brilliant and green and autumn burns
auburn
and amber and winter whitens with ice
on the waves
like a field while the holly grows red on its branch

here you have built two lives for love
while love in the living   comes true

George Elliott Clarke, O.C., O.N.S., F.R.C.G.S.

A revered poet, George Elliott Clarke was born in Windsor, Nova Scotia, near the Black Loyalist community of Three Mile Plains, in 1960. A graduate of the University of Waterloo (B.A., Hons.,1984), Dalhousie University (M.A., 1989), and Queen's University (Ph.D., 1993), he is now the inaugural E.J. Pratt Professor of Canadian Literature at the University of Toronto. Clarke has also taught at Duke University, McGill University, the University of British Columbia, and at Harvard University. He has also worked as a researcher, newspaper editor, social worker, parliamentary aide, and newspaper columnist). He lives in Toronto, Ontario, but he also owns land in Nova Scotia. His many honours include the Portia White Prize for Artistic Achievement (1998), Governor-General's Award for Poetry (2001), the National Magazine Gold Medal for Poetry (2001), the Dr. Martin Luther King Jr. Achievement Award (2004), the Pierre Elliott Trudeau Fellowship Prize (2005), the Dartmouth Book Award for Fiction (2006), the Eric Hoffer Book Award for Poetry (2009), appointment to the Order of Nova Scotia (2006), appointment to the Order of Canada at the rank of Officer (2008), appointments as Poet Laureate of the City of Toronto (2012-15) and as Parliamentary Poet Laureate (2016-17), and eight honorary doctorates. He is also a Fellow of the Royal Canadian Geographical Society.

John B. Lee

In 2005 John B. Lee was inducted as Poet Laureate of Brantford in perpetuity. The same year he received the distinction of being named Honourary Life Member of The Canadian Poetry Association and The Ontario Poetry Society. In 2007 he was made a member of the Chancellor's Circle of the President's Club of McMaster University and named first recipient of the Souwesto Award for his contribution to literature in his home region of southwestern Ontario and he was named winner of the inaugural Black Moss Press Souwesto Award for his contribution to the ethos of writing in Southwestern Ontario. In 2011 he was appointed Poet Laureate of Norfolk County (2011-14) and in 2015 Honourary Poet Laureate of Norfolk County for life and in 2017 he received a Canada 150 Medal from the Federal Government of Canada for "his outstanding contribution to literary development both at home and abroad." A recipient of over eighty prestigious international awards for his writing he is winner of the $10,000 CBC Literary Award for Poetry, the only two time recipient of the People's Poetry Award, and 2006 winner of the inaugural Souwesto Orison Writing Award (University of Windsor). In 2007 he was named winner of the Winston Collins Award for Best Canadian Poem, an award he won again in 2012. He has well-over seventy books published to date and is the editor of seven anthologies including two best-selling works: That Sign of Perfection: poems and stories on the game of hockey; and Smaller Than God: words of spiritual longing. He co-edited a special issue of Windsor Review—Alice Munro: A Souwesto Celebration published in the fall of 2014. His work has appeared internationally in over 500 publications, and has been translated into French, Spanish, Korean and Chinese. He has read his work in nations all over the world including South Africa, France, Korea, Cuba, Canada and the United States. He has received letters of praise from Nelson Mandela, Desmond Tutu, Australian Poet, Les Murray, and Senator Romeo Dallaire. Called "the greatest living poet in English," by poet George Whipple, he lives in Port Dover, Ontario where he works as a full time author.

www.ingramcontent.com/pod-product-compliance
Lightning Source LLC
Chambersburg PA
CBHW021439080526
44588CB00009B/605